# The Myth
# of Self-Esteem

# The Myth
# of Self-Esteem

## 50 Ways to Stop Sabotaging
## Yourself

**Terry Diebold,** M.A., M.Div.

Hado Press

ISBN-13: 978-0-9816604-0-0
ISBN-10: 0-9816604-0-1


Library of Congress Control Number: 2008905344


Book design and production by Tabby House
Cover design by Carol Tornatore

Printed in the United States of America

Hado Press
Fredericksburg, VA 22401

# Dedication

This book is dedicated to the loyal members of my Spirituality Group at the Women's Resource Center whose lives, struggles and triumphs define courage, and without whose urging, this book would never have been written.

# Acknowledgments

I would like to thank Eileen Boyd for her encouragement, and friendship and without whose help this book would have never come this far.

Also to Delise Dickard, Melanie Yost and Sonia Stevens, wise and gentle therapists whose thoughtful suggestions made the book ever so much better.

I also want to acknowledge my husband, Larry, for his constant and unwavering support over the years, and my children, Mike and Lindsey, not only for their tolerance of my brilliant ideas but also for doing most of their impersonations of me in another room.

# Contents

# Preface

Self-esteem is a never-ending topic of conversation. As a therapist, I have heard countless stories about peoples' lack of self-esteem. Yet, as I listened to these stories over the years, I was haunted by the sense that something just didn't add up. As I began to grope with the issue of self-esteem, I kept waiting to meet someone who had "it." My friends didn't; my colleagues didn't. *I* didn't. It simply wasn't there, at least not the way it was described. I began to explore the notion that we might have it wrong, this self-esteem thing. The more I talked about it with my clients, the clearer it became: our culture's sense of self-esteem is flawed. Eventually, what had been rattling around in my unconscious began to make sense. When people say, "I just don't have very good self-esteem," I tell them that they don't have low self-esteem because self-esteem doesn't exist. **Self-esteem, as defined by our culture, is a myth.**

The question isn't "What's wrong with *me* but, rather, what's wrong with *it.*"

When I say this to someone I can see what's going through their mind. *What? This is terrible. No self- esteem? There's got to be self-esteem. Quick, somebody haul this woman away.*

Self-esteem has become part of the self-help movement—a fad. What begins as a passing thought in someone's head is presented as

11

fact. Then fact becomes a movement and then the movement becomes Truth. The Truth is eagerly embraced and quickly becomes a fad and before you know it . . . Problem solved! Plagued no more!

We believe self-esteem is what we have been told it is and, now, a bastardized understanding of the concept has become Truth. Perhaps there are single and indisputable truths in mathematics and physics, but in this highly subjective area there are not.

By postulating that self-esteem is a myth, we are free to contemplate it in a new light. It is like looking through a prism at an ordinary object. It takes on new and magical qualities because its familiar colors and angles are transformed. This book is a prism that offers a way to rethink self-esteem. May it grant you freedom from the tyranny of not being good enough.

I wish you peace and wholeness.

Fredericksburg, Virginia

May 2008

# 1

# The Myth of Self-Esteem

*. . . The latest dates, discoveries, inventions, soci-*
*eties, authors old and new,*
*My dinner, dress, associates' looks, compliments,*
*dues, *
*The real or fancied indifference of some man or*
*woman I love, . . . These come to me days and nights*
*and go from me again, But they are not the Me my-*
*self.* [1]*—Walt Whitman*

Elizabeth sits on the office sofa, soft mascara tears streaking her
pale cheeks. Her nose is swollen and red. Today her dark, thick hair
is pulled back into a tight ponytail. There are no bangs, no curls,
just her stark face, twisted in pain. "It's no use," she says between
sobs, "I can't make it. No matter what I do, it ends in disaster. I will
never be anything but a failure. I hate my life . . . if it weren't for my
kids. . . ." Her voice trails.

Elizabeth's husband had announced unexpectedly that he was
divorcing her, and almost immediately transferred to Germany, leaving her less than three weeks to move out of military housing and
find another place to live. Taking the first job she could find, a part-
time teacher's aide, she makes less than $250 a week and with it

she pays rent on a tiny apartment, covers the bills and her attorney fees. She refuses to go on welfare.

"Elizabeth," I say softly, "what would have to happen for you to feel good about yourself?" She doesn't have an answer. Instead, she can only lament her sense of failure. "I'm a disappointment to everyone, including myself. I'm supposed to be happily married, taking care of a nice home, going places with the kids, helping out in their schools, making a fool of myself as a soccer mom. They should be going to music lessons and Scouts, playing with their parents in the backyard. Instead, they are trying to throw a football in our apartment's parking lot while their dad is playing catch in a grassy, fenced yard with some other woman's children." She collapses in sobs, rocking herself back and forth. This is not a woman mourning the loss of her marriage—she's well past that. No, this is a woman mourning the loss of her "self." Elizabeth feels as though she is dying but what she doesn't realize is that the part of her that is dying needs to be dead. That is the part that has her convinced she has failed. She is unaware that she is on the verge of discovering a self she never knew she had.

Elizabeth, like many of us, has defined her "self" by subscribing to someone else's idea of what she should be; she doesn't know that the self that lies hidden within her is superior to the ideal she embraces. It is not that Elizabeth has wasted her life—in fact, she has lived an honorable life. The problem is, she has done her best for everyone else except herself.

Sadly, this scenario is played out daily in therapists' offices, friends' kitchen tables and pastors' studies. This lack of "self" is found in workaholics and supermoms, aggressive behavior and in abusive relationships. It is found in introverts and extroverts, celebrities, and experts.

Men are not exempt from this syndrome either. There are strong expressions of failure in statements like, "I'm forty years old and still in middle management." Or, "I've been out of school for almost three years and I'm making less than any of my friends."

Self-Esteem comes from the Latin *aes* meaning ore (a mineral that contains metal valuable enough to be mined) and *tem* from the Latin *tomy* meaning "to cut." The word's etiology or origin is derived from the notion of cutting apart something valuable then appraising, estimating, summing it up. In other words, *aes* + *tem* means to open up and examine something that is valuable so it can be evaluated. *This* meaning actually comes closer to the true concept of esteem, which is a form of self-examination.

Instead of promoting thoughtful self-examination, our culture has created a myth about how we are *supposed* to feel about ourselves. This Myth has filled bookshelves with "How To" books and spawned endless therapy sessions. Parents worry about correcting their children for fear of damaging "it" while hiding the dirty little secret that they've never had "it" either.

The "it" is self-esteem. The Myth claims that something is wrong if you don't feel good about yourself. If you're unhappy, worried or doubt yourself . . . you have low self-esteem. This is bad, bad, bad. The Myth of Self-Esteem packs a double whammy when it comes to guilt. It says that not only are you suffering from low self-esteem but YOU ARE ACTUALLY THE CAUSE OF IT! If you only believed in yourself, these feelings would not be camped out in your psyche.

This myth leads you to believe that other people are happy, well-adjusted and confident. It alleges that self-esteem should be your faithful and ever-present companion, lighting the perilous path of life. All of our heroes have good self-esteem, fearlessly taking risks, indifferent to what people think of them. And here you are, cowardly, unsure, and pathetic, hating yourself for having so much doubt.

Self-esteem, as our culture understands it, is the cruel and eternal quest that one can never complete. Its very concept is grounded in the notion that things dark, unhappy and disturbing are bad. Failure is bad, mistakes are bad, feeling discouraged is bad, doubting yourself is bad. While we would righteously deny it, the fact is that we have zero tolerance for self-doubt. In a study cited by James

Tillman in his book, *The Myth of Family,*[2] the researchers found that children who come from "normal" homes tend to be less creative than those who come from disturbed homes. Tillman does not believe that dysfunctional homes are a good idea, but does see that problems can be the seedbed of creativity, not only from the standpoint of coping with them, but in utilizing their lessons throughout life. If we go back to the Latin definition that esteem is an examination for the purpose of forming a self-opinion, then we can dispense with the fairy-tale definition that self-esteem is feeling good about ourselves.

The other side of the "I should feel good all the time" coin is the equally mistaken belief that everyone else actually *has* good self-esteem. This is even more insidious because self-doubt is all the more unbearable in the face of others' success.

Elizabeth, the woman we met in the opening of this book, looks around her world and only sees people who are happy and doing well; she sees them fulfilling *her* dream.

At worship, everyone is happy and smiling. At school, pleasant-looking moms happily cut out brightly colored alphabets and smile proudly during teacher conferences. At work, co-workers get promotions and raises. What Elizabeth does not see is the pain and disappointment behind the masks that these people wear.

This is a common, distorted thought that lies at the base of much of the misery surrounding the issue of self-esteem. Elizabeth must face her true nature, a humanity where doubt and uncertainty dwell. She doesn't grasp that this is what it feels like to everyone. When we are hurting, we think we are the only ones who ever felt this way; we are convinced that other folks haven't failed and never get discouraged. The intriguing thing is that most of us would probably deny that we feel this way. We pay lip service saying, "Of course other people get discouraged," but secretly we really do believe we struggle more than others with these feelings.

We also think that other peoples' mistakes are temporary, understandable and forgivable but that our mistakes are permanent, unfathomable and unforgivable. The bottom line is, it seems, that others *fail* but we are *failures*. In reality, they are looking at us saying, "Why can't I get my act together like Suzie or Tom?"

Where did we get this mistaken notion of self-esteem? The idea, while not new, seems to have burgeoned with the Boomers. Frankly, my grandmother could have cared less whether anyone had self-esteem. She was too busy raising five children during the Depression after the loss of her husband. In an effort to correct the perceived harm done by their parents, Baby Boomers have gone to great lengths to heal themselves of the scars inflicted by the "damaging" child rearing practices they endured. Phrases like "Why can't you be smart like your brother?" to "You hit her again and I'll rip your arm off and beat you with the bloody stump" have driven an entire generation to reparent itself.

This desire to be perfect is the delight of Madison Avenue. We are brushed, fluoridated, deodorized, pressed, creased, washed, and moussed; educated, analyzed, politicized and socialized. It is as though we are run through a cosmic car wash, disinfected on all surfaces with metaphoric mops and foam. Our personalities are waxed and buffed so that when we emerge, we present a polished face to the world.

About twenty years ago a new television show, *Northern Exposure,* turned out to be a surprise hit. The premise was that a New York medical student who accepted financial aid from the state of Alaska found that he had to serve as a doctor—not in Anchorage as he though—but in obscure, isolated Cicely, Alaska. What made the show so appealing was the eccentricity of the characters. Not everyone was *liked,* but everyone was accepted.

In Cicely, people were able to be themselves and were not consumed with impressing each other. The doctor was selfish and petulant, the celebrity was arrogant and manipulative, the wife of the tavern owner remained an eternal teenager and the pilot was chronically unclear about how to be in a relationship. No one had "poor self-esteem" because no one felt compelled to compare himself to someone else. The characters battled their strange and sometimes negative idiosyncrasies, not because they felt inadequate or ashamed, but because they wanted to be better people.

The allure of this show was that it was like watching ourselves. These were familiar problems being encountered by people like us. We watched them struggle with each other, act foolishly, and face the truth about life and themselves. Deep within, we long to let it all hang out, to "be ourselves." We do not necessarily long to be told we are wonderful and that everything we do is great because we know it isn't true. We do, however, long to be accepted as we are, including our faults and fears. We want very much to know that we aren't "less than" just because we are picking our way down the rocky path of self-doubt. We want people to tell us that their child didn't make the team either, that they didn't get the promotion, and that they don't exercise. It is not that we want others to struggle; it is that we are comforted when we find out that they do.

What does this root translation of self-esteem, to examine ourselves, have to say about success? After all, isn't our goal to be successful? When we scrutinize ourselves, if we aren't successful, our opinion of ourselves is negative. There is good news, bad news here. The good news is that we live in a culture of achievement. The bad news is that we live in a culture of achievement.

Achievement, per se, is not the problem. The problem is that achievement and success are ideas run amok. They have taken on a life of their own and have a singular meaning: more, more, more. Achievement and success have become *the* goal. They have become the final destination, not just stops on our journey.

In the global world that comes into our homes so matter-of-factly, we are now in competition with millions of people, not just the Joneses. Not only have we been led to believe that everyone else can do it better, but that usually someone got there first and *already* did it better. There is an enormous temptation to let thoughts such as these paralyze us. There is no mythical goddess to give us the magic sword with which to slay this dragon. There is no warning that the quest to go higher is an endless, insatiable task and that the higher we climb, the larger the mountain becomes.

Those who have reached the pinnacle—gold medal, Miss America, Pulitzer Prize—if they are lucky, will find a way to make these gifts meaningful beyond their face value. The rightful endowment of achievement is the deepening of life. Too often in the hoopla of glory and celebration, there is no time for reflection, leaving all tinsel and no tree. If we can stand on the other side of our struggle and understand its significance, then our moments of discouragement will reveal persistence and courage. For many of us, our victories are clouded. We turn our heads slowly, hoping that we will not see what we know is there, the ugly, gnarled gremlin of our alter-self, the critical and negative heckler spewing out the murky sewage of self-doubt. Our ever-haunting fear is there, taunting us: "You're not good enough."

When things go wrong, and we have to talk ourselves into feeling good over and over again, it is like rearranging deck chairs on the *Titanic*. Our transformation must occur at a deeper level; what must change is our core belief about ourselves. We must recognize that we are not alone with our flawedness; we must be okay with not being okay.

# 2

# The Failure of Failure

*How far high failure overleaps the bounds of low success.* —Sir Lewis Morris[3]

*The spirituality of imperfection begins with the recognition that trying to be perfect is the most tragic human mistake.* —The Spirituality of Imperfection[4]

FAILURE.

The word itself is laden with accusation. It is not perky and its very pronunciation is rather drawn out <sup>Faaillll</sup> <sub>uuurrr.</sub> It hangs in the air in leaden silence. In fact, we actually try to avoid the word in an effort to soften bad news: Bob's business "went under;" Sally has to "repeat" the course. Very unpleasant, this business of failing.

Just as it does with bad breath, yellow teeth and cellulite, our culture springs to neutralize failure. When our failure is only moments old, we are advised to "Focus on the positive, you'll have another chance, the world will not end, you will live to fight another day." There are books on how to conquer failure and step-by-step programs to get over it. There is soothing self-talk and forgiveness to get through it. Sales manuals burst with ways to avoid it.

Despite the best efforts of our society, failure is still with us! It is with us in big ways and in small, everyday ways. Failing is so natural a part of life that, try as we may, we simply cannot avoid it. We can't ignore it so we do the next best thing; we co-opt it. We wrap up it up and tie it off with cheerful ribbon. It becomes one of life's little inconveniences from which you can bounce back if only you have the "right attitude" and "don't let it get you down." Failure is something to overcome, conquer, vanquish. Like going to the bathroom—everyone experiences it but no one discusses it.

We've heard the stories about famous people who failed. There was Colonel Sanders who failed eight times before he successfully launched Kentucky Fried Chicken. There was Babe Ruth, the Home Run King, who, five times led his league in strikeouts. These are, indeed, wonderful examples of overcoming failure but they miss the point. The point is that *failure is essential.* It forces us to reach deep into our soul to make sense of things and eventually neutralizes the fear that immobilizes us.

The Myth of Self-Esteem lures us into thinking that failure is shameful. The reality is that failure draws us inward and grounds us in our humanity. It gives meaning in a way that happiness cannot. Failure, in all its darkness produces shadows and just as shadows create depth in paintings, failure creates dimension in the otherwise flat canvas of our existence.

If you can sit with failure, you will notice things that success prevents you from seeing. When plans don't go as expected, failure gives you a chance to stop running, catch your breath, and face your own potential. Failure does hurt, but that doesn't make it a bad thing. Embracing failure, like exhibiting courage under fire, confers strength and dignity, metaphoric medals that commemorate honor in the face of battle.

Georgia O'Keeffe, a renowned but unconventional artist of the last century, found herself in a failed marriage. This was particularly painful not only because she lost her husband to another woman but because for decades she had scandalously flaunted the highly erotic relationship she enjoyed with her husband, Paul

Steigliz. It was not uncommon for Georgia and Paul, in the midst of a family picnic, to race upstairs to their bedroom, laughing and stumbling, making no secret of their intentions. Later, O'Keeffe was subjected to the same behavior when Steigliz flagrantly cavorted with his paramour. O'Keeffe, powerless to stop the affair, remained "captive" as a spurned wife in New York City, a place she never wanted to go in the first place and that to her was a prison.

The year was 1942 and women rarely left unhappy relation-ships. O'Keeffe did. Despite her disappointment and humiliation over the affair, she packed up for New Mexico and there began the most prolific and creative period of her artistic life. Her "failure" gave her new eyes to see the world around her. She acknowledged pain; she did not run from it, excuse it or glamorize it. It was her companion, greeting her in the morning, tucking her in at night. She gave it space and allowed it to stay and do the work of deepen-ing her life.

A life that denies reality and marches ever optimistically to-ward happily-ever-after is ultimately an unsatisfactory life. The pursuit of a life untarnished and dreams unblemished creates a world of successful people who have failed. When someone refuses a challenge, it is an attempt to avoid the fear, shame and disillu-sionment of failing. The irony is that people *do* sense the impor-tance of risk, but cannot free themselves from the cultural encap-sulation that insulates them from heeding the call to their creative selves. Risk is a weighty endowment that keeps us grounded and living consciously.

Jeff's young face reveals deep crevices between his brows. Slouched over, his hands clenched together, he stares at the floor. Every now and then he runs his fingers through his coarse, curly hair. Finally, he looks out the window and sighs.

"Ellie's been great. She knows I love working for the paper even though evenings are shot and we don't get much in the way of ben-efits." He shakes his head.

"I feel like I owe Ellie and the kids more. Her parents are pretty well off . . . she's used to having more than I can give her. Our friends are buying houses, building their 401Ks and here we are renting, not much in savings. Then, here comes this job. . . ." His voice fades.

Last Tuesday Jeff had been offered a better paying job with full benefits. The only problem was that it was in a large city. He and his wife were happy where they were, close to relatives and friends. His job at the local newspaper kept him involved with the community and provided him varied opportunities from reporting to layout. The new position was editor of a national trade magazine. It was work he was capable of, but it was not the newspaper business he loved. His internal voice was clamoring that this was his big chance. "Everyone has to move sooner or later," the voice reasoned. "Think of what the kids could do and see in the city. You could finally afford to take a real vacation, buy a house with a big yard!"

Jeff was perilously close to making a decision that would deconstruct the life he loved. It would substitute a life that, at best, would be vaguely dissatisfying and at worst, lethal to his spirit. Jeff sensed that he didn't want to go, yet couldn't elucidate why, since on the surface, his proposed "new" life sounded better. His fear of making a mistake distorted the real challenge, staying with a job that made him happy.

Had the circumstances been different, had he felt stifled in his career, the challenge would have been to take the new job. In that case, staying where he was out of fear would have been safe and would never allow him to respond to his "soul's code,"[5] his vocation.

There is an old adage that says, "Good judgment comes from experience and a lot of that comes from bad judgment."

You get numb to constantly wounding your soul. You learn to ignore the warning signs of depression, anxiety, apathy. You fold your dreams neatly and put them away because you can't fit into them any longer. Smoothing the wrinkles out of your hopes, you place them at the very bottom of an old trunk in an obscure corner of the attic. Someday you will kneel in front of the trunk, pull them out and hold them up saying, "Once I wanted to," your voice trailing off like your life of unworn dreams.

How do you cope with disappointment when you can't accomplish everything you want to do? It's not possible to achieve everything you want but your soul knows what is important and will let you know. What is significant and what ultimately matters is that you try. When fate calls to your soul and you turn your back, you deny your purest essence: your potential. Deepak Chopra says, "When you discover your essential nature and know who you really are, in that knowing itself is the ability to fulfill any dream you have because you are the eternal possibility, the immeasurable potential of all that was, is and will be."[6]

Your potential is nurtured by risking failure. Your potential, to paraphrase an adage of Winston Churchill about kites, " . . . flies highest against the wind." You cannot allow the specter of failure to clamp chains on your ankles, shackling you to a wall of regret. Something that does not turn out as you expected is a disappointment; regret means you never tried.

Veterans who are praised for their courage often say they were terrified of the battle ahead but went on anyway. After staring down death, they say, everything else seemed easy. What they learned was perspective. In facing failure, the relevant perspective lies in the importance of trying. You may fail but you will not be haunted by the regret of never trying.

Finally, there is the matter of your own integrity. If you have ever turned down an opportunity fearing criticism if you fail, or been goaded into taking an unnecessary or dangerous risk because you don't want anyone to think you're a wus, you know what it is to be disappointed in yourself. Self-respect comes when you have done your best and listened to yourself. It comes when you have shut out the clamor and judgment of others. It comes when you are honest with yourself and make your decisions with reverence for the sacredness of your potential.

When you begin to live your life consciously, putting aside your fear of failure, you will find that when your spirit begins to reemerge, it will be like someone stumbling out of a cave into the sunlight, blinking against the brightness of the light. Your life will become a contemplative journey, not a linear dash for the goal line. This sense of your deeper essence has, most likely, been buried under layers of distraction and fear. Living in a personal world where failing is not only okay, but necessary, rests on responding to your purpose and substance. It heralds the banishment of the endless measuring stick. It is the beginning of wholeness.

In the New Testament it says that our yoke is easy and our burden is light (Matt. 11:30). This means that what we want to do is, or will become, our passion. We will not dread it. We are not meant to be a square peg in a round hole. We are given the gift of desire and the skills to fulfill that desire. The work we are called to do is exactly the work the world needs us to do. Our soul will find peace when we follow our heart.

# 3

# Soul and Spirit

*I believe in you, my soul . . .*[7]
—Walt Whitman

Why is our literature so enduringly rife with reference to the soul? Ancient Greek texts refer to it, Shakespeare is laden with it and poets would be hard-pressed to pen many poems without mentioning it. Through thousands of years, the soul is universally recognized as the profound expression of human essence.

"It is my soul that calls upon my name."[8]

Why does this quote from Shakespeare capture this fascination we have with the soul? The answer is at once simple and complex.

From the beginning of time humankind has always believed a powerful force governed the world. From offering sacrifices to a golden calf to worshipping in great cathedrals, humankind has acknowledged its lesser nature. We reach up to "It" out of a deep longing to connect with this presence which is greater than ourselves. We know at our core that we can only be completed by the Transcendent, and we know intuitively that this connection cannot be made by our corporeal selves.

While we respond physically by building altars and performing rituals, what we really want is to accommodate this place within us that yearns to be united with the sacred. We reverently set this place aside and honor it because we know that it is true and we know that it is here, alone, that we connect with the Ultimate, with God. It is our soul that is the seat of our spirituality and it is our soul that comes closest to uniting with the mind of God.

Yet at the same time that we are conscious of the Ultimate within our soul, we also must be conscious our soul's humanity. Thomas Moore in his book, *Care of the Soul*[9] explains that while our spirit is where we aspire to loftiness, our soul is the human, grounded part of us. Through our soul we experience life with all the wonder and excitement of a child. Our soul is the holding environment for uncertainty and confusion, but also for playfulness and delight. It experiences the warm sand between our toes and the salt in our tears. Weeping and darkness coexist with laughter and light. They are entwined in such a way that to ignore or mismanage one is to do the same to the other. We are largely conscious of the religious implications of the soul, but are not as aware of the human essence of our soul. It may seem strange to speak of two seemingly opposite notions, spirituality and humanity, residing simultaneously within the soul. This is because we are woefully ignorant of the absolute and utter oneness of our mind, spirit and body, yet the soul is not conflicted. Both sides of our soul need connection with the Numinous. "My soul is satisfied as with a rich feast . . . my soul clings to you."[10]

We might pay attention to that part of our soul that is connected to the Sacred by going to church, synagogue or mosque or spending time in nature or helping the poor. But as we go through the daily motions of living, it is the human part of our soul that we ignore. Why? The answer is, simply, because we *can.*

We ignore our soul because it does not send dunning notices and it does not charge interest on what is overdue. It doesn't schedule mandatory meetings and it doesn't give grades. When the soul first signals that something in our life needs attention, it whispers in a tone so hushed that with just a bit of busyness or distraction, we are deaf to it. Because the soul is not measurable or visible, we don't make the connection between it and our physical world. We are culturally hypnotized into thinking that if something is not tangible, it doesn't exist. If it doesn't exist it has no standing in our world of grocery shopping and report deadlines. When we ignore any part of our soul, we find ourselves out of balance and feel at odds with ourselves although from the outside, at least for a time, everything appears to be fine.

When our soul begins to cause trouble and forces us to acknowledge this imbalance, we usually turn to science. But even science realizes that problems are not necessarily fixed with pills. There are a growing number of scientists who acknowledge the spiritual realm and do not find it at all in conflict with science. In fact, many scientists and doctors consider the mystical to be an integral component to life. One only has to note that Harvard Medical School now publishes a newsletter centered on the relationship between medicine and spirituality to attest that spirituality is a mainstream concept.

Accepting the concept that it is the soul rather than the mind or the body that "needs" is fundamental to personal peace. We have to understand that ignoring the needs of the soul is certain to cause problems. Our Puritan heritage makes it difficult to tend to the human side of the soul because we think that it is frivolous or self-serving to respond to something so intangible.

About this time someone usually says something like, "My soul tells me I need that Mercedes over there," but we all know that's facetious. Your soul may be speaking to you when it tells you that if your mind is so tired it cannot think a cogent thought, you are not honoring the sacred within you. Or, it may be trying to warn you that when you won't allow yourself to try snorkeling because it is too darned expensive that you may be saving money but squandering the renewal you so desperately need. We need to understand that some physical needs, like tiredness or restlessness, are warning signs that we are spiritually on empty.

As we move through our mortal world, we habitually fail to recognize the price we pay when we ignore our soul. Restlessness and depression are the calling card of the soul ignored. Mental and physical symptoms soon emerge as the result of our inability to balance the concrete with the spiritual. When we place too much emphasis on the physical, we get further and further away from those unpleasant messages that our soul may be trying to convey to us. When we place too much emphasis on the spiritual, we drift from reality. Sometimes we just freeze, knowing something is wrong but are afraid to act because society does not recognize, much less embrace, the spiritual gift of uncertainty. Being at peace during disquieting times is alien to our culture. Better to be in a panic than to ask the meaning of our uneasiness and doubt.

When do you decide to act or not act? When should you "do" and when should you just "be"? The following prayer answers this question.

### The Serenity Prayer
Lord, grant me the serenity to accept
the things I cannot change,
The courage to change the things I can,
and the wisdom to know the difference.

This tells you that there are choices you need to make when you act. One thing is certain: If you do not accept yourself *where you are,* you cannot make effective choices to listen to and balance your soul. You end up busying yourself with superficial issues while ignoring the unsettling plea from within.

If you are doing poorly at work and face the possibility of being fired, concentrating your energy to find a more efficient route to work is not going to increase your performance. Confronting your lackluster performance is physically and spiritually healthier than methodically sabotaging yourself until the proverbial axe falls.

When Thoreau wrote "most men [people] lead lives of quiet

desperation," he acknowledged the universal feeling of being trapped in a dead-end life with no appreciable way out. Meaningless lives are lived by people who have no hope in themselves or their world; they hear their souls yet are disconnected from them. The only thing they are connected with is the ache for something that is missing.

I see this disconnect in clients who come in depressed and hopeless. Their despair is based not only on the fact that their lives are not turning out like they want them to, but on a pervasive feeling of helplessness. The diversions they have pursued to expunge that feeling—work, drugs, sex, status, food—have not helped. In fact, this quest for happiness only intensifies the feeling of hopelessness because they have looked within and found no resources to confront the abyss.

When people examine their emptiness, they inevitably end up saying, "I've never had good self-esteem," because they assume that this emptiness is unique to them. They think that if only they had good self-esteem, they would no longer feel empty and worthless. They believe that self-esteem is the magic ingredient in a wonderful, carefree life.

What Western culture teaches is that these darker parts of us—doubt, fear, failure, envy—are rueful, keeping us from a life of bliss. In reality, they are part of the yin and yang of the Self.

The Chinese, in the philosophy of I Ching, believe that all change in the universe can be explained in terms of opposite principles called yin and yang. For instance, cold is yin, heat is yang. It is believed that these opposites give rise to each other; therefore, within success is the seed of failure, within failure is the seed of success. Since yin and yang principles occur on a rotating basis, no one principle is continually dominant.

This philosophy encompasses the mysteries of existence much more so than Western thought. When yin and yang work in harmony, one is balanced and life is predictably unpredictable. However, with the expectation that life will be stable, people panic, thinking

31

their life is a cosmic catastrophe when things go wrong. It is crucial to understand that troubling feelings are not aberrant but rather counterbalance and complete us. We should expect to cycle through these feelings as a normal consequence of natural law. Our soul may be troubled during these times but it will clearly tell us what it needs to become balanced.

During my first semester in college, I was lying on my bunk, in a deep depression, wracked with gulping sobs. I remember saying to myself, "I wish I could be like my roommate, Peggy." This was because Peggy was amazingly even-keeled and never seemed unhappy. Then, in the midst of my grief, I had a revelation: I realized that Peggy was never really sad but she was *never really happy*, either. She went through life, one day pretty much like the last, no highs, no lows.

I saw that expecting things to be on an even keel, "shushing" a laugh that is too loud or a cry that is too shattering, reinforces that we are not okay when we are feeling. When we strive to be acceptable we often talk ourselves out of feeling alive.

I knew at that moment, lying there about as miserable as anyone could get, I wouldn't trade one moment of my misery for her, dispassionate, level life. My life was different after that. I realized that there is price to pay for passion and joy and I was more than willing to pay for it.

This shadow side of our soul, the part that allows doubt and shame to reside within us is like the allegorical albatross in Samuel Taylor Coleridge's "Rime of the Ancient Mariner." In this story of a becalmed ship, an albatross flies through the icy fog and brings with it a good south wind to return the ship to its course. But the mariner didn't give the albatross time to bring good luck. Instead, he killed it because he thought it was the reason the ship had become becalmed. For his punishment, he was forced to hang the dead bird around his neck. Our culture, as did the Ancient Mariner, has shot the albatross. Like the fog that enveloped the ship, fear and uncertainty obscure our ability to discern meaning. We misread these aspects of our soul, underestimating their role of propelling us to create, mold and refine our Self, seeing them as the albatross, foreboding failure. We symbolically destroy our albatross by ignoring these feelings. Our punishment is the heaviness and stench of fear as it hangs from our neck, like the murdered bird hung about the sailor's neck.

The very odor and presence of the dead bird was the sailor's punishment for destroying a good omen. It was his rejection of the omen that caused the ship to become becalmed, just as our rejection of our shadow Self stunts our journey of growth.

When we reject this less conventional side of ourselves, not only do we prevent self-actualization but we also reject the dark portion of our soul that is essential to our authenticity. The longer we pretend that we have no insecurities or faults, the more insecure and defective we feel. Success and achievement feel hollow because deep within us we believe we are deficient and have managed to hide it only temporarily, misleading people into thinking we are competent. When we pretend we have no insecurities, we sweep an entire part of ourselves under a metaphysical rug and place a piece of furniture over it. This is the "Imposter Syndrome."

People who have achieved a fair and sometimes large degree of success in their lives and feel that they don't deserve it, experience this syndrome. They are afraid that if people really knew them, their success would be exposed as a fluke, a shameful puddle of lies and fakery.

These persons have spent so much time whistling past their psychic graveyard that, even when successful, can hardly stand to take credit for their achievements. This denial of self, both bad *and good,* is rooted in the Myth of Self-Esteem and directly affects our soul.

When people are convinced that uncertainty, fear and doubt reside in everyone and that these emotions can impart great wisdom, they will no longer look over their shoulder for fear the "truth" will catch up with them.

The Myth of Self-Esteem helps us ignore our soul. Any time we ignore our soul, we begin to compensate in unhealthy ways. In *Care of the Soul*, Moore points out that the soul ignored is a soul in pain. "Emptiness, meaninglessness, vague depression, disillusionment about marriage, family and relationships, a loss of values, yearning for personal fulfillment, a hunger for spirituality. All of these symptoms reflect a loss of soul.." (page. xvi). [11] We experience a loss of soul when we try to squeeze our spiritual self into a box not meant for us. We experience a loss of soul when we compare the imperfect person within us to the perfect person we believe others are.

Up to this point all we have talked about is our soul. But, is there a difference between our soul and our spirit and does it really matter? According to Moore[12], while the soul is more sensual, the spirit is the more intellectual component of our spirituality. It prompts us to better ourselves, to read worthwhile books, to do something for humankind. Ultimately, our soul feels but our spirit understands. Our soul experiences but our spirit assigns meaning. Our soul is our personality, our spirit our conscience. The soul is untouchable; it is enclosed in a place within us that remains intact despite devastating circumstances. Our spirit, on the other hand, is vulnerable; it can be influenced and undergo change. Our soul *is*, our spirit *becomes*. Our soul can't be crushed but our spirit can be broken.

We need to care about both soul and spirit and make a grave error if we cater to one but not the other. Tending the spirit without being mindful of the soul creates judgmentalism and self-righteousness. It isolates us from feeling which creates distance from our own humanity and others'. Tending the soul while ignoring the spirit promotes selfishness that blinds us to the needs of others.

There may be those who are confused and perhaps offended at the thought of differentiating between the soul and the spirit, believing that God is slighted in this definition. But our soul and our spirit are godlike, both responding in their own ways to the Sacred, becoming sacred in the process.

In the Christian religion, God chose to become human in Jesus. This Jesus possessed a soul that was divine but it was at the same time human because he experienced anguish and disappointment. It was Christ's soul which felt the agony the night before he died but it was his spirit that accepted the death he knew was coming. The soul is holy in a human way because it is our core; the spirit is divine in a numinous way, claiming its place in the Sacred. The Holy Spirit, on the other hand, is the very consciousness of God. It contains the thinking of God, the mind of God. When a person prays to be filled with the Holy Spirit, they want the essence, the soul and spirit of God to reside within them. Both soul and spirit bear the imprint of God.

Other religions may not speak directly of the soul or the spirit, but they acknowledge that the totality of humankind cannot be contained wholly in the body and believe that the spiritual is greater than the corporeal.

Undistorted self-love accepts all that comprises the soul and spirit. There is nothing to "overcome" because there is no disgrace in imperfection; yet, at the same time, there is always room for growth. Healthy self-love means there's a place for critical self-examination and redirection, and provides the checks and balances when evaluating behavior. The belief that there should be no imperfection is what impairs our spirit and our soul. It is only when we love and accept ourselves that we are able rise to our truest calling, to love deeply and generously accept our fellow human beings and their faults.

# 4

# The Myth of Independence

*No man is an island, entire of itself.* —John Donne

The Myth of Independence relies heavily on Western thinking as epitomized by the John Wayne School of Self-Worth. Our culture has predetermined the parameters of success by defining it in terms of self-reliance, independence, raw courage in the face of immovable circumstances, and a stiff upper lip.

Misplaced self-reliance is the mistaken belief that a person is weak if they need help. While it is true that we should not expect someone else to meet all of our needs, it is not true that turning to others is weak. This belief is hard on males since culture does not stigmatize women for asking for help.

The joke that the Israelites wandered in the desert for forty years because Moses wouldn't ask for directions is a tongue-in-cheek depiction of the effect this myth has on men: Real men don't stop and ask for directions. But why? Why is it so bad to stop and ask directions? Because it proves you don't know everything! And if you don't know everything, then you aren't as smart as the next guy and before you know it, you're feeling stupid. But stop and think about it—where is it written that we are supposed to know everything? It is written on our hearts, to paraphrase a line from the Bible. What should be written on our hearts instead is that the world is too big and too complicated for us to know everything. That's why there are maps and gas stations. While there are those who want someone else to bring purpose to their existence, for most of us the overarching message is: "Do it yourself."

Oh, we know we can't move a piano by ourselves, but do we really understand that we can't go through life by ourselves? Do we really understand that acquaintances aren't the same as friends? That having close friends makes us better, encourages us to give from a deeper place and helps us finally share the secret things that have gnawed at us and kept us isolated?

From the beginning of time, women looked to each other for companionship and solace when men, the hunters, were gone. Women raised their children together, cooked together, and performed rituals together that created loyal and trusting ties. Even as late as the early 1900s it was not unusual for several families to live in the same house, with women sharing the housekeeping and child-rearing chores. While it is true that men also did things together, like barn raising, by and large these events were specific and limited.

Women have traditionally spent more time with children than men and it is no secret that the bond between mother and child is the most enduring of all relationships. The poignancy of this bond can be heard in the stories of soldiers, dying on the battlefield, crying, "Momma, Momma," in their delirium.

But even in the mother-child relationship, the Beast of Independence rears its judgmental head. Despite the cultural imperative that mothers "be there" for their children, women are later chastised for not being able to "let go" of their children when they get older. Mothers worry when their kids wobble down the street on their first two-wheeler and when they go on their first date. The clear message to women is that they worry too much. While there are men who wait up for their kids, more often I hear that it is the mother who cannot go to sleep until the child comes in and the husband who complains: "Just go to sleep—if something is wrong we'll hear about it. You're babying him/her." The underlying hypothesis of this attitude is that dependency is bad. What's wrong with this picture? What's wrong is the fact that being concerned about the people we love is viewed as unnatural!

This is not about encouraging someone to become helpless through dependency. This is about understanding that we cannot do everything by ourselves, that we need each other in various ways and innumerable times. The Myth of Independence bullies us into believing that to need help is weak and therefore there is something intrinsically lacking within us if we do. In short, we are a dependaphobic society.

Even with the good start that women had huddling in the caves together, we have managed to do away with the concept of interdependence among women and replaced it with . . . Supermom! A Supermom! does everything herself because she "should" be able to go to work, attend school plays and ceremonies, work in her community, church or synagogue, exercise, floss and maintain a meticulous home with pies cooling on the window sill. A Supermom! doesn't ask for help or if she does, it is either sporadic or grudging. She says yes when she should say no and is exhausted even if she does manage to get enough sleep (new studies show that women get an average of two hours less sleep a night than men). Unlike her grandparents and great-grandparents, she feels guilty for not being able to live up to the image imposed on her by the likes of Martha Stewart and furthermore feels she should do all of the homemaker stuff *and* work outside the home.

Men are not exempt either. Many are driven by the dread of not succeeding, sacrificing priceless moments with their children to put in overtime. They fear being perceived as soft, as not being a team player. To object, to say they want to spend time with their kids, is viewed as being weak and under-motivated. They learn to ignore that need to reconnect with a family they haven't seen in four nights straight. They ignore the numbness that creeps over their spirit so they are spared the pain of impaling themselves on the company flagpole.

While in seminary I did a study on emotional intimacy. It was unscientific and primitive, but very telling, nonetheless. At first I was going to tape interviews about emotional intimacy with men and women, but quickly found that while I was able to obtain interviews with women who told incredibly poignant stories about experiences they had with parents or children, I couldn't find any men who would consent to be interviewed. Finally I found a male therapist who agreed to do it, but when the questioning started, he talked about the intimacy issues that come up in therapy! He had no intention of talking about any of his own experiences with emotional intimacy.

I decided to use a different approach to the research, and did a blind survey about emotional intimacy. Again, it was crude and statistically unreliable, but sadly remarkable at what it revealed. With one exception, it was not hard to separate the male responses from the female. When men described their feelings about intimacy they used words such as "exposed" "vulnerable" "uncomfortable" "confined," while women used words like "spiritual" "closeness" "connectedness" "comforting."

True independence is balanced by emotional intimacy, close personal relationships and the ability to ask for help. Even those who claim they feel great and don't need anybody are living out of only half of themselves and that half is on the surface. There is a decided sense of nakedness when independence is the only clothing you wear.

The deepest desire we have is to be loved. This makes the concept of independence tricky business because loving and being loved inherently requires another person. According to the American definition of independence, the "evolved," self-confident person should be capable of providing his or her own validation, which is absolutely true. Our self-worth should not depend on someone else's opinion of us. But this is not what loving and being loved means. Wanting to be loved is about connection and meaning. We experience wholeness when we are in relationship with someone whom we love and trust. This connection grounds us and prevents us from becoming self-involved. It creates a more expansive personal world that teaches acceptance of others and ultimately lays the groundwork for forming community

The benefit of living in community has been debated throughout history, most notably by religious hermits, known as desert fathers, and monks who chose to live apart from their communities. These men (although history records some women hermits) spurred by the desire to become closer to God, banished themselves to places that were inhospitable at best, uninhabitable at worst. In these conditions, without human contact, these hermits fasted and prayed, unencumbered by daily distractions. The desert fathers were highly esteemed by the church, regarded as true ascetics who sacrificed themselves for God. They are often regarded as the people with the answers, strong enough to give up pleasure and human contact. But despite the depth of their conviction, it is questionable that a life lived in isolation is a meaningful life. Some might say that a solitary life could be a full life but, by definition, a full life is a life that takes advantage of what the world offers—beauty, meaning, joy, helping others and making a difference.

One of the gifts the world offers is the gift of each other. Humankind is set apart from animals by its ability to assign meaning. You can have a meaningful moment, but it is deepened when it is experienced with others. A concert attended by one person cannot match the excitement and appreciation of a theater full of people. Interestingly enough, this is true not only for the audience members but for the performers as well. While they are perfectly capable of creating the very same music whether before an empty row of seats or the whole auditorium, every one of them will tell you there is a measurable difference when playing for an audience.

We will never know the reasons some people want to live wholly without others. Modern psychology and medicine tell us that a person may become a recluse as a result of a chemical imbalance or the absence of proper bonding during early stages of development. Either way, not connecting is abnormal, yet culture persists in implying that isolation is desirable when it is rugged independence.

This is not to say that on any given day, each of us doesn't fervently wish to be removed from the company of people who are making life miserable. This is a normal reaction to being surrounded by negativity, criticism or simply too many people, however loving they may be. But these are temporary inconveniences, not a lifestyle.

Why all this talk about intimacy and love and relationship if this is a chapter about the Myth of Independence? None of us is truly independent; acting as though we are cuts us off from the very lifeblood of being human—needing and being needed, not feeling alone, asking for help, experiencing another human being in a meaningful way. We have been conditioned to *avoid* intimacy because then we might eventually *need* someone.

There was a much-publicized mining accident that left nine men trapped underground for three days with water gushing around them. As the water levels rose and the hope of rescue dimmed, the miners tied ropes around themselves so that they could die together. These men were tied together, mentally, emotionally and spiritually and it probably saved them as much as the rescue effort because together they had hope; they were able to comfort and encourage each other and no one feared dying alone in the dark.

We must learn that being alone is not a measure of who we are. *How* we are together is the measure of who we are.

# 5

# Lost and Found

*No! I am not Prince Hamlet, nor was meant to be . . .*
—T. S. Eliot

"I feel out of place." "I don't fit in." "I've always been different."
While these comments may sound like they are from individuals
who are uncomfortable with themselves, feeling out of place is common. Once again the Myth of Self-Esteem makes us believe that we
are the only ones who feel this way and that there is something
wrong with us if we do.

When you don't have a sense of who you are, you are more
likely to feel disconnected from the world. As you give yourself
permission to explore some of your "bad" feelings, you will grow to
know who you are spiritually, and eventually, you will feel grounded
even if you find yourself in an uncomfortable setting. You will feel
"in" your place; you will know why you're where you are and the
significance of it.

Feeling lost affects us on both an emotional and spiritual level.
Lacking a sense of place results in an uneasy, insecure feeling, because unconsciously we feel we are missing out on being a part of

something universal, more cosmic than ourselves. We are not unhappy but we are not exactly happy either as we try to shake off a muted sense of emptiness.

The concept of place consists of four areas: 1) community, 2) geographic location, 3) emotional connectedness and 4) spiritual belonging.

## Community

Belonging to a community is intrinsic to understanding and claiming our role within that community. Next to our family identity, it shapes our fundamental selfhood. Years and miles away, we are grounded by who we were in that community and how it felt to be a part of it as we were valued by friends, neighbors and family. Sometimes that foundation is a negative one where community represents betrayal and disappointment. Either way, community imprints us for the rest of our lives.

For some, like military families, community is temporary; yet even brief bonding with their group will have the same effect on their sense of belonging. "I'm an Army wife or a Navy brat," these persons might say. What they mean is that they identify with other people who have to make many places their home and who learn to feel comfortable in places where they are strangers. They know they are all in the same boat and from this shared experience connection is built. To someone who travels or who never had an established childhood home, the world becomes their community, expansive but at the same time welcoming, as they realize that people share a universal sameness greater than their differences. Community is not always dependent on geography but it always requires people.

## Geographic

The second component of Place is geographic. Someone may have a persistent desire to be in a particular place even if he or she has never been there before. Some people, when they see the desert or mountains for the first time are filled with an overwhelming spiritual connection to it. It may seem like they've been there before or that they are finally "home." Either way, they are overcome with a deep awareness that this is where they belong.

A guest on a television program featuring Shakti Gwaine, the author of *Creative Visualization,* described this phenomenon. He lived in a city but had a vision of a place where he would finally be "home." He could not say where it was but it was beautiful and lush and definitely not in a city. Years later he visited Hawaii and by chance happened to take a ride to a little-known section of the island. As he rounded a curve on the dirt road, he saw it, the place he saw as home—exactly as he had pictured it. He knew at that moment that this is where his soul already lived. Through a series of unlikely events, he acquired this expensive property despite having limited financial assets. He never went back to his apartment in the city. His desire to remain there was so strong that he sent for his things because he knew he had found his spiritual place. His soul, spirit and body were home. In this man's case, his spiritual place also happened to be his geographical place.

Geographical place is what makes you feel connected in a global sense. A physical place can link you to other cultures and enlarge your sense of participation in universal humankind. Something you did not even know was within you is awakened. It can challenge you and lead you to new paths in your life, like moving to a big city and discovering your creative element in its hustling energy.

Sometimes your geographic place is not somewhere you can be all the time, like Africa or China, but this place speaks to you unlike the other countries or places you have visited. Something resonates within and suddenly you know where you fit into the world community and how you are connected to these people you have never seen before and may never see again.

For others, geographical place may carry a memory from another time in their life. It might be as tangible as grandmother's kitchen or as ethereal as the smell of burning leaves. What is important is that whatever form the geographical location takes, its importance lies in giving us a place where we can affirm our sense of belonging.

We must listen to this need for place because claiming "home" grounds us in the self that sprang from its roots. Being connected with our place fills us with the security of belonging and emboldens us to challenge life with curiosity and passion.

## Emotional Place

Emotional place has to do with a sense of being grounded and comfortable with who we are. But *being* comfortable is not the same as *feeling* comfortable. Being comfortable with ourselves means knowing there are times when we won't feel smart or accomplished. It means there will be times when we feel angry or stupid or sheepish.

Obviously this is a difficult task if you think you can't make mistakes. If you fall victim to the Myth of Self-Esteem, you will think that you are the only one who has made a fool of yourself. If you listen to stories of people who are admired or who have accomplished extraordinary things, you will find that they looked foolish, were maddeningly stubborn or ticked off a lot of folks on their way to greatness.

Picture Louis Pasteur, the man who discovered germs, telling people that they have crawly things all over their hands that could make them sick and, oh, by the way, germs are INVISIBLE. He couldn't even convince physicians to wash their hands before surgery. It might be safe to assume that people thought he was nuts. It was only after the number of deaths from infection began dropping after doctors began washing their hands that his theory gained credibility. Had he kept his theory to himself for fear of sounding stupid, a lot of people would have died and who knows how long it would have been before someone else made the discovery.

Pasteur wasn't worried about his self-image; he knew he was a good scientist, that his theory made sense and that it would be important for the world to know about it.

Emotional place is where our soul resides. It is a source of our intuition and inspiration, that place inside that responds to what happens to us. It is the terror we felt when we were seven and got lost. It is the pride we felt when we made our first dollar; it is the birth of our children and the death of our parents. It is jealousy and anger, selflessness and selfishness. It is mature and at the same time childish. It is the truest part of us, the part we know to be our essence, the distillation of who we are.

When we ignore this part of ourselves or conform it to someone else's image, we are out of emotional place. When we trust ourselves, we do not need someone else's paradigm of emotional place because our emotional center is balanced and in touch. When we feel we must become something we're not, we perform the basest kind of psychic self-mutilation. Over time our emotional place becomes so distorted that it often takes a life-changing event to jolt us back to ourselves, to make us remember who we once were, who we were supposed to be.

This should not be mistaken for an "anything goes" blessing. The compass in your emotional center keeps you faithful to your soul and spirit. It is when you are threatened that you resort to behavior that is self-destructive; by this I mean not only hurtful behavior but actions which belie your true self, like becoming an engineer when you are an artist, having children when you don't want them, going for the money at the cost of your soul. It is a denial of God's gift of Self. You deny yourself the joy of fulfilling your soul's calling and deprive the world of your best work. While being out of one's emotional place is sometimes not immediately evident, eventually it sounds a death knell for the soul.

## Spiritual Place

Spiritual place, while still very personal, is larger, outside of us. It is that place in us that gives our lives meaning; it is more than we can be alone. Our inner wisdom knows that our spiritual place is part of a creation that is inestimable and transcends the world as we know it.

While spiritual place is similar in many ways to emotional place, it is more about how we fit into the bigger picture and our connectedness to that which is outside of ourselves. Of course, how we fit into the bigger picture is dependent on our emotional well-being. A serial killer is quite obviously out of both emotional and spiritual place and it is not surprising that many serial killers are drifters who either never had a family life or had a bad one.

What comprises our spiritual place? Our spiritual place is our nature, is in God, is our connectedness, is our need to give and receive. It encompasses those we know and those we don't yet know. It is history and art and beauty. It is darkness and evil. It is free will and dependency. It is the yearning to be essential, it is knowing that you count. It is being valuable. It is realizing you are but a small part of the world yet equal to anyone else. It appreciates all humankind. Hatred cannot cohabitate with our spiritual place.

This spiritual realm is all around us at every moment. We can choose to acknowledge and participate in it or not.

Hardened people do not understand the spiritual realm. They only know the concrete and the provable and they honor only the jagged edges of living that cut and tear the soul. People who do not have a sense of place in the spiritual world cut down trees that take hundreds of years to grow. They don't care if a species becomes extinct. They think the appreciation of art and music aren't really necessary in schools and that money is more important than people. They are arrogant in their rejection of things that cannot be proven or seen. They are the center of their own creation and are, in essence, Bob Cratchit in *A Christmas Carol.*

Dicken's character did not believe in any of the qualities that are found in spiritual awareness. And like Bob Cratchit, individuals who have bought into the Myth are out of spiritual, communal and emotional place. Feeling good about themselves is measured by a distorted yardstick of power, money and prestige. The rewards of goodness and fairness are cemented over with the need to control, to be recognized, to be better than.

Some time ago there was a news story about a factory, Malden Mills in Lawrence, Massachusetts, that burned down in 1997. The third generation owner of the factory, Aaron Feuerstein did a remarkable thing. He could have just taken the insurance money and retired—after all, he was seventy-one. Instead, he pledged that all 3,000 employees would continue to receive their paychecks and insurance benefits while the mill was being rebuilt. He offered this to his employees without fanfare, without seeking media recognition or praise. He felt a social responsibility, imbued in him by his father, Sam, who told him, that where there are no people of moral correctness, he should act as if the entire world were resting on his shoulders. "You've got to do it all yourself," he would say, "You've got to make it happen."[14]

Some of these employees came from generations of family members who had worked in the mill since his grandfather bought it in 1906. He understood that the ties he had with them were morally and spiritually binding. The simple virtues that this man exemplified earned him something few employers today experience: the loyalty and respect of his employees.

Aaron Feuerstein knew his spiritual place—Provider and Protector. He did not listen to the established mores of industry that would have essentially said to these employees, "Too bad." He chose the path which was true to his spirit.

It may sound as though there's no room here for capitalism. Quite the contrary. Without money, wonderful things could never be possible. Diseases are cured and charities are funded through donations given by people who have created wealth. It is not about how much money you make, but about how you make it. As yourself some simple questions. Are people's rights being violated in order for you to profit? Is anyone being harmed? Are people getting hurt? Are you listening to your conscience? Do you feel that what you are doing is positive and part of a larger plan for humankind, whether it's working on a cure for cancer or simply being a good employer?

There is one last element within our spiritual place that we cannot ignore—the dark, shadowy side of our soul. Helga Newmark, sixty-seven at the time of the interview, was the first female Holocaust survivor to be ordained a rabbi. When asked about Anne Frank's famous statement that all people are "really good at heart," she replied, "There is good and evil in all of us. If we can accept that, then we can accept it in ourselves and then we can accept it in others and take the necessary precautions against evil."[15]

Acting as though you don't have the capacity for evil within yourself makes you dangerous because when your dark side creeps out, you will be shocked and unprepared to deal with it. Like weight training, exercising vigilance over the possibility of your capacity for evil will strengthen your power over it. While most of us, thankfully, will never have to face profound evil within ourselves, we face the seeds of it at home or at work when we dehumanize others, give in to hatred or look the other way when wrongdoing occurs. The Myth of Self-Esteem raises the stakes for success, creating a "wining is everything" mentality. The Myth robs you of your initiative to see the truth and destroys the internal mirror that is so important in accepting and dealing with the baser parts of yourself.

The fact that the potential for evil is present does not mar the concept of spiritual place because spirituality encompasses the totality of our being . . . body, soul and spirit.

How do you know if you are in the spiritual place that is best for you? The best test is to ask yourself how connected to yourself and the world do you feel? If you are honest with yourself, you will know whether you are connected or disconnected. If you are struggling or feel alienated, left out, friendless or lonely in a crowd, it may be a sign that there is an internal conflict. If you are distant from other people, you are probably distant from yourself, not allowing feelings or refusing to acknowledge destructive behavior. Feeling a spiritual, emotional, communal and geographical sense of place is analogous to having a sacred dwelling place. If we have no place to call home, we become wanderers, emotionally and spiritually rootless. We will constantly seek but will not know what we seek. We will have no North on our compass, will not know how far to go or if we need to stop and rest. We will not know who we are. This makes us vulnerable to someone else's definition of who we should be.

The serenity we seek is around and within us. We need only be open to what draws our soul and spirit to know where we belong.

# 6

# The Twinship of Passion and Creativity

*Go out in the woods, go out. If you don't go out in the woods, nothing will ever happen and your life will never begin.* —Clarissa Pinkola Estes, *Women Who Run with the Wolves*[16]

Passion and creativity are gossamer strands that weave enchantment in and out of our imagination. Through them, we interpret our world symbolically, transforming our lives into sacred vessels that hold the mysteries of the universe. Creativity is the nucleus of our life spirit and unless we are mindful of it, we mutate into flat, joyless beings.

Our soul is the fertile earth of imagination, carrying within it the seeds of our creativity. Each of us yearns to participate in the creative process and each of us longs to give form to the ideas that take shape in our souls. Our reason for being is to transform these ideas into the embodiment of our vision. These elements of imagination cannot be separated; passion is as vital to our creativity as blueprints are to construction.

People have always loved stories about heroes and what draws us to these heroes is our identification with their passion. Heroes usually start out reluctant to face their challenge but fate intervenes, leading them to discover their passion. Some heroes are lead to tragic bravery and some to greatness, but eventually, each leaves a mark on the world.

Christopher Columbus overcame his own fear and the ridicule of others to test his unshakable theory that the earth was round. First century martyrs endured unspeakable torture and the Pilgrims endured unrelenting hardships to establish a society where they could worship in freedom. Monet and Gauguin painted out of their passion, refusing to conform to the "rules" of art. Her passion for the dying poor brought world attention to Mother Teresa, making it possible for her to establish her communities worldwide.

We are deeply moved when we share someone's creativity because it is the sharing of a soul. When we identify with someone's creation, it comes from the universal experience of creativity. We intuitively feel what the artist felt when we view the *Pieta*, read *The Old Man and the Sea* or heard the *Hallelujah* chorus. We are moved by the passion of the poor black woman who took in laundry for sixty years . . . then donated $150,000 for underprivileged black student scholarships. We are grateful for the creativity of "simple" things when we eat a home-cooked meal or sink into a feather bed, cozy under the weight of a handmade quilt.

Within us, we have the capacity to distinguish our own vision. We have the ability to think creatively about problems and devise solutions that doggedly evade others.

What we hold within us we can express through our innate ability to create. Children yet untouched by the Myth show us the connection between creativity and self-worth when, after laboring intensely over their creations, they hold them up for all to see. What they are really saying is "Hey! I'm Good! I'm somebody unique. I can do things." It is in the bringing forth that we connect with ourselves, find our best, understand our bond with the cosmos and know at a solemn level that we are important in the majestic scheme of creation. It does not matter if what you create is obscure, unrecognized or undervalued. It will affect someone; it is needed by someone. The world would be a lesser place if it was cheated out of your soul's gifts.

The Myth of Self-Esteem goads us into looking over our shoulder when we create. "I'd be laughed right out of the room if I entered this photo in the contest. . . . I can't sing in front of all those people." We compare ourselves with others, decide what we have done is not good enough and pronounce ourselves insignificant. The Myth steers us into the belief that our creative efforts can only be validated by recognition and wealth. The simple fact is that most of us won't be recognized that way. The majority of us will live ordinary lives, doing ordinary things in ordinary places. It is against a backdrop of ordinariness and everydayness that our creativity paints a swath of color, breathes life where there is suffocation, provides a new vision of hope. It is not about us . . . it is about responding to our call, which affects the quality of life and wholeness of others.

Our destiny impacts others' destinies and their destinies affect others' destinies and so on. When we deny our passions, we cheat others.

The bird does not think about why it sings—it sings because that's what birds do. It does not matter if anyone is listening because a bird's song is innately beautiful—its gift to the world. A cat's job is to do as little as possible yet it is this very characteristic of cats that we love. Their nonchalance, the way they sleep, the way they ignore us—these are the gifts of cats to us. When we come to understand that it is *our* essence that makes others' lives richer, we take the first step in undoing the damage that the Myth has done. The essential quality of our soul, ordinary though it may seem to us, is substantial and significant. What we create is not solely ours but must also be shared with the world. Some people, when they think about this concept for the first time, say they lack passion for anything, that since what they "do" doesn't amount to much, they have nothing to contribute.

Not having passion is the result of living in a one-dimensional world of work and obligation. When a person lacks the desire to have fun and be creative, it considered to be a sign of depression. Buried under the Myth of Self-Esteem, people don't believe their interests are creative because they seem ordinary. A passion for scouting or sports, for gardening or working on cars, a passion for children or pets or nature . . . these are all gifts awash with creativity that should be shared to enhance the lives of others.

When you don't pay attention to your creative urges, you lose sight of your significance. Unlike the child who loves herself and her creations, you are not able to step back and admire your work saying, "Because this creation of mine is unique, I am unique. This creation of mine is good and that makes me valuable. I make the world a better place and that means I make a difference." It doesn't matter if you are a little frog in a big pond because it is neither the size of the pond nor the size of the frog that matters. What matters is that you are divinely designated to contribute something fundamentally essential to this planet and when you respond to that call to passion and creativity, you are fulfilling your destiny.

How can you tell if you are creating? If you have ever "lost" time while doing a project you are creating. If you have looked up and four hours have passed or you were so absorbed that you forgot to eat, you are creating. When you are creating, time is suspended because you are so captivated that it feels like you have been transported to a different dimension, a dimension of ideas and absorption in the creative process. Obligation, responsibility, schedules, deadlines—all disappear when we are in our creative selves.

There is no end to the things that qualify as creative. Creativity is inspiration to do what you love, where ideas move forward into form. Creativity regularly beckons us but often we are deaf to its call. We become immune to our needs and think that spending time doing something that is not "productive" is wasted time.

A number of years ago a magazine ran a small but interesting article about an elementary school teacher who believed so firmly in the power of creativity that he conducted an experiment with his students He wanted to see if giving them "creative time' would positively affect them. He took them outside everyday and had them lie on the ground, look at the clouds and just daydream. At the end of the school year his students' scores were higher than other students in the same grade, even though they all started out with basically identical scores. Of course, this wasn't a scientific experiment but the outcome was well worth it. The students felt better about themselves, had more energy and were more successful in problem solving.

What this teacher discovered is that time thinking about "nothing" is profoundly important since creative time nurtures energy and imagination. Daydreaming allows the mind to break free of convention. When a group brainstorms, no idea is too improbable—anything goes. Eventually the collective creativity of the group results in unusual or resourceful ideas that would have never emerged from a dry, structured staff meeting.

Another example of the power of creativity is the toy company that regularly schedules playtime for its adult employees. They are encouraged to play, throw things, be silly, laugh; the result is the company is recognized as producing some of the industry's highest productivity and employee loyalty. The leadership of this company understands that our culture does not encourage us to embrace our creative selves but rather pushes us to conform. Unfortunately this is so common that there probably isn't a person reading this book that at one time or another hasn't been afraid to introduce a new idea for fear of being ridiculed.

When your creativity is suppressed or ignored, you become a caricature of yourself, a one-dimensional character who lives in a flat world. You are poorer for the loss of yourself and the world is less magnificent for the loss of you. Like a puzzle with one piece missing, the absence of your passion and creativity leaves a space.

To find time to create you have to commit to making time. I

know, I know, you're saying, "How?" How when you work two jobs? How when you are a single parent of four children? It will never be easy. A solitary activity that needs concentration may have to take place in the morning before anyone else is up—or at night or when the phone stops ringing. You must fight for your time and plan for it in your schedule as you would a doctor's appointment. If you have no energy during the week to do one more thing, then take time on your day off. Sometime—maybe even most of the time, it may be impossible to squeeze in creative time, but at least let yourself daydream and do not allow busyness to be an excuse for a life not fully lived.

How do you start this process of "unleashing" your creative self? It has to do with how you do things. If you are constantly "on task" there will never be time. There will always be bills to pay, shopping to be done, clothes to wash, cars to fix. Something will always be there to suck the life out of you. You have to break your routine to realize how programmed you are—and it produces ruts that smother creativity. Introduce yourself and your children to paints and canvas and take a lesson from them—they will not be intimidated. Eat chili for breakfast. Buy a different brand of soap. Go home a new way. Take a picture of something you like. Let the dishes sit. Go for a walk. Part your hair on the other side. Sit in a difference place in church. Buy shoes if you only wear sandals; buy sandals if you only wear shoes. Turn the TV off. Get a sketch pad. Play with clay. Skip a meeting. Go barefoot. Eat a whole bag of popcorn then skip dinner.

This is your life and it is your only life. If you could see your life from beginning to end, you would see how much time you wasted on things that were not important. Creativity and your passion for it is the seedbed of your self-worth. You have innate value by virtue of being born. You can nurture yourself and the world at the same time by honoring your desire to create. No matter your age or what you have done up until now, there is still time to achieve your creative impulse . . . but you must start now.

# 7

# Family Matters

"The more we cling to the overriding importance of parents and the more cosmological power we accord them, the less we notice the fathering and mothering afforded by the world every day in what it sends our way."—*The Soul's Code*, James Hillman[17]

Choosing our friends but not being able to choose our family is like a poker hand. Some of us have a full house, some of us have crap and some don't get any cards at all. The cards we are dealt, however, are not a measure of how good a poker player we are. It's what we do with the cards that counts. Our family absolutely influences our lives but it is not a measure of who we are and does not have to decide our fate.

You may think that only those who are born into poverty or abuse face difficult challenges in their lives. This is not necessarily so. A few years ago Oprah interviewed Maria Shriver about her success as a broadcast journalist. Maria Shriver, despite having an excellent education, faced reverse discrimination in her first job as a reporter because her boss was convinced she was a spoiled rich kid who got the job through family connections. Maria told of coming in early, staying late and taking assignments no one else wanted in order to win the respect of her colleagues.

You could argue that she was brought up in a home where everyone was successful and that by example she learned to deal with adversity. And I'm sure to some extent that is true. But, even the best of families can generate expectations that adversely affect their children's character. Privileged kids may think the world is waiting breathlessly to offer them a fat job with lots of vacation time. They may think they are above the law. These beliefs result in socially crippled persons who are just as unable to function in society as those who come from deprived circumstances.

On the other end of the economic and emotional spectrum, we find Oprah Winfrey, born poor and black in the South, who was sexually abused and had behavioral problems. But, there she was, the most successful woman in America, on her own top-ranked talk show, chatting with Maria Shriver. Both women are successful because they both worked hard to overcome obstacles originating from family circumstances. The conundrum here is that there are no absolutes when it comes to predicting what effect family will have on someone. In fact, James Hillman, in his book, *The Soul's Code*[18] argues that family can actually have little effect on people because each child's destiny is written on his or her soul. This destiny, according to Hillman, will emerge, regardless of family. There are many who would argue with Hillman, especially teachers and therapists who see the destruction wrought by family dysfunction, but ultimately the debate is an old one: Is a person formed by nature or nurture?

Transactional Analysis, a theory of psychotherapy developed by Eric Berne and more commonly known as the "I'm Okay—You're Okay" theory, examines the messages or, as he calls them, injunctions, we get from our parents such as "Don't Be Close, Don't Be Happy, Don't Be Smart, Don't be a Girl . . . Don't Be."[19] Most of us play out our lives according to the role we were assigned in the family until one day we figure out that the mother who imparted the message "Don't Be Close" had a problem with intimacy herself or the father who relayed the message "Don't Be Smart" was afraid he would be humiliated by a son who is smarter. It is life-changing when we grasp the fact that we don't have to live out the identity our parents imprinted on us.

When we understand that parents, who view life as well as their children through their own psychological pain, will convey tainted, prejudiced messages, we are released from invisible bondage. It is like waking up to find you are not only healed but were never handicapped in the first place. You are not lazy or stupid or ugly. You can amount to something, you're not a burden. You begin to realize that *you* must choose your own message to yourself. You can believe that you aren't as smart as someone who is wealthy or you can conclude that wealth does not matter. You can become the worthless person you were told you were, or you can value yourself and reject your family's pattern of verbal abuse or ignorance.

Loyalty is another issue that poisons family dynamics. Clients speak to me of the difficulty of going against their family's "plan" for them. They feel like traitors because they decided to reject their assigned role.

It *is* painful to parents when their child decides to do his or her own thing. A professor I once had told a story that lightheartedly illustrates this phenomenon. This guy was right out of the How To Dress Like a Professor manual. He had a beard, horn-rim glasses, the ever-present turtleneck and a tweed sport coat with suede patches on the elbows. His hair was rakishly disheveled, he was never without his pipe and his office was scattered with books and papers. He also used a lot of words I didn't understand. At any rate, he told us that he had taken his four-year-old son shopping for new clothes. The boy was immediately drawn to a rack of mini-suits, complete with collar shirts and little ties. Bow ties. Try as he may, the professor could not dissuade his son from picking the clothes that were the antithesis of his image and, obviously, the image he wanted to cultivate for his son.

Family loyalties can be dangerous. A child (or grown adult child) will sometimes be ostracized or "taught a lesson" when they will no longer participate in the family culture that, for instance, includes gossiping or racism. It can cause family cutoffs when children refuse to buy into what are considered positive family expectations, such as church, frugality or driving a sensible car.

A healthy family will recognize that their children are individuals and will not necessarily do what the parents and siblings would like them to do. Unhealthy families will deride family members who reject their communal values or won't go along with the job or career that the family want for them.

An example of this occurred when I was in graduate school. A school counselor had referred a high school senior to our clinic. During the previous three months his grades had steadily declined and he gradually became depressed. He agreed to come to the clinic but was terrified his family would find out because they disapproved of counseling.

What eventually emerged was that this young man had been offered a full scholarship not only to college, but also to medical school as well. Basically, he was brilliant but no one in his family had graduated from high school let alone college. Like the rest of his family, it was expected that he would to go to work as soon as he graduated from high school. He loved his family and it was clear they loved him. Yet he knew how important these scholarships were. At an unconscious level, he thought that if his grades dropped, the scholarships might be withdrawn and he would not have to choose. He realized that the consequence of following his dream to be a doctor was rejection by the family. They chided him saying, "Do you think you're better than us, going off the college? Once you're an important doctor, you'll look down on us." The injunction he was getting from his parents was, "Don't be successful."

Extreme? Very. But this is played out everyday in some respect in hundred of households. The boy did finally accept the scholarship, but at great cost to himself. Through counseling he was able to differentiate himself from his family and decided not to embrace the role he had been given. He chose to reject the messages he had been given and give himself new messages: "Be yourself. Be smart." Once the family saw they weren't going to change his mind, they realized they had two choices: They could embrace him or lose him. They chose to embrace him, appreciative, eventually, of his talents and proud of his achievements.

Sometimes the loyalty problem isn't as obvious. This was played out by the engineering student who couldn't seem to finish graduate school. He had been working for almost to three years and still hadn't done his thesis. His family was increasingly upset with his seeming inability to concentrate and get his degree. In desperation, he went into therapy where he admitted that he really wasn't interested in engineering. He had continued because his dad was an engineer and had dreamed about the day when his son would join him in his engineering firm.

You can probably guess what the problem was. Because he didn't want to be trapped in a career he would hate, he unconsciously sabotaged himself. If he never finished, he would never have to face the fact that he was making the mistake of his life. Here was a good son who respected his father who was a good and caring man. Because of this, the price of disappointing his father was too high. While he didn't know this on a conscious level, he was willing, on an unconscious one, to live with nagging dissatisfaction for what appeared to be the rest of his life rather than to differentiate from his family. The influence of his family, like that of the young man who wanted to be a doctor, was keeping him from believing in his own potential. In both cases the young men were asked to fulfill themselves with someone else's view of what and who they should be.

What does all this have to do with the Myth of Self-Esteem? It has to do with someone else's ability to rob you of yourself. What is more insidious is when the family, both as a unit and as individuals, falls for the Myth. In the case of the first young man, his family's identity was that they were "plain folks" who distrusted education and felt threatened by it. Why should they support or trust a culture that doesn't respect them because they have not been successful by its yardstick?

If a disingenuous notion of what is worth respecting weren't so firmly entrenched in our culture, all occupations would have dignity. Today, being a sanitation engineer or a waitress is viewed as a marginal job that should be performed by people who could not do "better." If each of us was respected for who we are rather than what we do, there would be no need for the young, aspiring doctor's family to circle the wagons to keep "them" out. They innately recognize "them" as people who judge and look down on them. If their son were to become a doctor, he would become one of "them."

In the case of the young engineer, he, too, is a victim, by proxy, of the Myth. His father wanted to spend more time with his son and pass the business on to him, but his father also knew he would be viewed as successful when his son chose the same occupation. This would validate him as an engineer and as a father. It had become clear to the son that Dad would be disappointed if he didn't achieve his father's dream.

These two families don't define what it means to be a family but do illustrate the deep, hidden influences, both positive and negative, that lurk in the quest for self. In an ideal world, family members would feel valued because they are recognized as individuals with special gifts and talents. Unfortunately even this simple message can be distorted into identifying gifts and talents primarily as a means to recognition rather than a gift to benefit the individual and society.

If you are a gifted artist but take advantage of people in order to get ahead, then no matter how good you are, your talent is ultimately wasted. If you achieve everything legitimately on your own but do it for the ultimate good of just yourself, you will soon hear yourself saying, "Is that all there is," a syndrome that takes up residence in people when they have achieved everything but feel empty inside.

The grace and beauty of honoring one's talents reminds me of the night we hit a deer on a dark back road in rural Michigan. The front end of the car was completely smashed in and we could hear some mechanical thing under the hood scraping against some other mechanical thing. Obviously, we were not the kind of people who could fix mechanical things. With smoke and steam hissing from the front end of the car, we limped into a small town that earlier had simply been a dot on the map. We pulled the car into the lone gas station (closed) in town and parked it. The only motel was open so we headed for it and fell into bed, shaken by the accident. We also worried about being stranded on a holiday weekend with a foreign car (this was Michigan . . . home of the Motor City, the *American* Motor City). The next morning when we walked down to the gas station, we were surprised to find a dark-haired man in overalls working under the hood of our car. Introducing ourselves, we expressed surprise that he had begun work on our car. "Well," he said from under his baseball cap, "I eyeballed the front end of the car and knew right away what happened since we get a lot of folks like you hittin' deer and all.

"It was plain you was on your way and needed to get the car fixed. I said to myself, 'Fred, you need to get these people back on the road so's they can git where they were headed in the first place.' Figured you was plannin' on gittin' there last night so I started on it first thing. Made you a piece sump'in like the one that broke. That oughta hold you till you can get it fixed proper. I pushed the grill out so you could drive it. She's ready to go." We were dumbfounded. After thanking the man profusely, we paid him even though he said we didn't owe him anything and went on our way. Later, when we took the car to the dealer, the mechanic said that whoever rigged the part was pretty clever—he doubted he would have even thought about fixing it that way.

This man knew he had the ability to make a difference—he knew his gift lay in his inventiveness and mechanical knowledge. He probably knew he was appreciated for who he was because people who understand their worth do what they love and do their best work, not to impress or receive a reward but simply because they can. They are self-possessed and have a sense of place and purpose. It is natural for them to be generous, not looking for recognition but accepting it when it comes. Their self-ness comes from their connection with themselves and how they relate to the world around them.

This gifted man was not stingy with his talents and knew he could make a difference; recognition and praise were not the basis of his actions or being. His confidence grew out of the fact that he did not measure himself against anyone else's yardstick; he was not competing with anyone else to guarantee his self-image; he was not struggling with himself.

Up until now we have been looking at people who outwardly seem successful but are at odds with their family's goals for them. But there is another familial role where the person appears willful and self-serving: the role of the "black sheep." Black sheep don't care what their family or society thinks. They stubbornly proceed to thumb their nose at everyone by doing exactly what they want. This does not refer to the person who wants to mooch off others while he or she does nothing. This refers to the person who doesn't do the safe thing, who follows her soul's call. People who follow their heart are dangerous people. They make us face ourselves and our self-delusions and ignore a culture that idolizes personal success at the cost of their souls. Ignoring the Myth, they refuse to let it sap their life and spirit with oughts and shoulds and can'ts.

By refusing to take the "safe" road, Black Sheep may be venturing into areas that will reveal truths to them they may not like. They are like the character in the film *Soylent Green* played by Charleton Heston. The movie is a futuristic depiction of an ideal society. But Heston, instead of blithely following everyone else in lockstep with the program, slips into an area he is not supposed to see. He discovers the awful secret about the food that is provided by the benevolent overseers who manage every aspect of his society. They were recycling the dead into food. When he makes his discovery, he runs outside horrified, warning his fellow citizens, screaming "Soylent Green is people."

Black sheep are the brother who won't go to college because he wants to be a musician or the mother who races stock cars. These are the people who refuse to go quietly to their psychic deaths. They refuse to become fodder for other people who want to blot out the awful truth that it is they, not the black sheep, who have lost out.

If we are honest with ourselves, we would have to admit that we are secretly jealous when someone takes a risk, with no guarantees that what he or she is doing will even remotely work out. We are jealous because it reminds us of all the roads we have not taken. We want the risk takers to be like us and follow the rules. Then we are assured that they are in the same boat we are, a boat that doesn't want to be rocked.

This is not another indictment of the family because our families are as much casualties of the Myth as we are. True, there is no diabolical plot to ruin our lives but our culture has little patience with uncertainty and intuition, with imaginations that color outside the lines. Our only reprieve is to understand that everyone has doubts and life is messy. Sooner or later everyone turns down an opportunity that could have changed their life for the better. But we can rise above mediocrity when we decide that there are times we will not turn away from the struggle. We will step into the unknown and untested, knowing that struggle is necessary for growth.

When you take full responsibility for yourself and for your decisions, good and bad, you will begin to understand. You will understand that if your family was screwed up, you go to counseling, if you were poor, you get a job or a scholarship or an apprenticeship. You will understand that it is scary to do something that isn't guaranteed, that things don't always turn out well, that you won't always be liked. Family matters *do* matter. It is all in how you allow them to matter.

# 8

# Metaphysics, the Universe, and Love

*Love is the divine madness.*—Socrates

Of all our relationships, the ones in which we experience or expect to experience long-term sexual and emotional intimacy have the potential to impact us as much as our family-of-origin experiences. The influential nature of these relationships is based on the fact that, unlike childhood experiences where we have no choice as to whom we are with, in intimate relationships we participate as adults and are, therefore, responsible for our choices. In addition, sexual intimacy exposes us to a vulnerability unlike any other type of relationship. The Myth of Self-Esteem has a profound impact on our understanding of these relationships and our expectations of them. To add to this, our ability to choose a life partner depends on how we view ourselves. If we don't view ourselves in a positive light, it can complicate a loaded and already complicated process.

As Helga Newmark, the first concentration camp female survivor to become a rabbi, said in chapter 5, "There is good and evil in all of us. If we can accept that, then we can accept it in ourselves and then we can accept it in others and take the necessary precautions against evil."[19]

Recognizing that we all have shortcomings is foundational for making good choices in partners. It is not that we are looking for someone without faults. It is that we are looking for someone whose faults will not strip us of our dignity and crush our spirit. Dr. Harriet Lerner has created a brilliant criterion for judging whether or not a relationship is healthy. She proposes asking yourself this question: *"Does this person make my world bigger or smaller?"*[20]

This is the $E=mc^2$ of relationships. If a person, no matter how loving, doesn't want you to expand beyond their limits, this person is bad for you. THIS PERSON IS BAD FOR YOU.

This is not to say that even in good relationships there won't be problems when one partner changes. If you decide to leave a lucrative career in the stock market to become a chef, this will profoundly affect your family's income. With some soul-searching (to make sure of your motives and stamina for such a drastic change) and careful planning, a career shift can be made. Sometimes the sacrifices are drastic, such as selling the house, living on half an income, or going back to work. Sometimes they are more subtle like putting in long hours or getting used to the loss of prestige.

Predictably, symptoms are likely to emerge when adjustments such as these are requested of a partner; jealously, anger, suspicion, resentment or grief, to name just a few. A period of adjustment occurs before a partner can settle into acceptance and begin the task of supporting something new. Sometimes a partner may need therapy to help them through a rocky time such as this.[21]

These are all normal reactions in a relationship during a period of change. Give and take, a respect for each other's growth and an absence of competition for superiority or domination are all signs of a healthy relationship.

There are, however, relationships where a partner feels threatened by growth. The partner who isn't threatened finds herself in a constant battle to maintain Self. She is subjected to a stream of messages designed to make her doubt herself, her contribution, her place or her rights in the relationship. There is also the partner who cannot trust. She tends to make selfish and unreasonable demands, begrudges a spouse's successes, criticizes and denigrates her partner and creates roadblocks that prevent him from pursuing his interests, studies or travel. All of these behaviors are designed to do one thing: *Prevent a person from embracing his or her life.*

People who have to control are persons who fear rejection and abandonment. They fear that if you have new experiences or are exposed to different ideas and new people, you will see the scope and consequence of their inadequacy and leave them. They know you will leave once you discover people will treat you better than they have. They're afraid that you will meet people who are more interesting, more respectful and more encouraging, and you will come to the realization that you have little freedom in the relationship. They are terrified that they will not measure up or that their controlling behavior will be exposed for what it is and you will reject them. The old expression, "keep 'em barefoot and pregnant," is code for "We don't have to treat them well if they don't know any better." Despite the obvious reference to women in the previous quote, this also goes for women who try to limit their male partners.

The Myth of Self-Esteem cuts two ways in this case. People have a need to control because they want to feel powerful. They don't feel powerful because they don't believe that anyone would want them. Their behavior is a calculated means to an end: Be in control at any cost because if you aren't, no one will stay with you. This person embodies such profound emptiness that any threat, no matter how small, looms as absolute and immutable disaster. The anger in a person this devoid of self is frightening. Either they lash out so threateningly that their partner acquiesces or they become profoundly depressed, threatening or suicidal. The goal in all of these cases is the same: Control.

Concurrently, the partner who continues in a controlling relationship does so because she either doesn't have the confidence to handle the situation or has a high need to be needed. She believes that if she is not in a relationship she is a failure. But above all, she is afraid to be alone. Afraid of what it feels like to live with herself and afraid that with no distractions, she will see herself as she really is, spiritually and emotionally impaired, unable to fill her own empty spaces, needing someone else to transfuse her with their energy and life force.

She is afraid that if she left, no one else would want her. The person who is being controlled is so ashamed of staying in an abusive relationship that in order to cope, she views herself as a victim rather than taking action. She also fears that other people will view her as a failure if she can't "keep" a man so she continues the cycle of self-doubt and abuse.

The saddest reason of all, however, for staying in a relationship like this is unfortunately the most common. These people who stay are so frightened of the void that they would rather be in a bad relationship than none at all.

If we remain in denial about any of these facets of our own character, we will end up in a sick relationship that destroys not only us, but our children. It is not at all unusual for someone who grew up in an alcoholic family to marry an alcoholic, divorce them and then marry another alcoholic. The same pattern occurs in abusive families. Some of these children, later in life, either tend to marry an abuser or become one themselves. It is not always the case, of course, but this is a well-documented family pattern.

Those who make the same mistakes over and over again in their choice of partners need counseling. They must recognize and understand that they are attracted to partners who are abusive or disrespectful because they have not worked out these issues within themselves.

This darkness that dwells within controlling partners is dangerous to the point that the fear of who they are *not* becomes deadly. These insecure and abusive people are shadows of themselves, so barren inside that in order to tolerate daily living, they must psychically absorb their partner. Like a peacock spreading its feathers to attract a mate, a controlling person can be charming and wonderful in the beginning. This is because at an unconscious level he thinks that no one would even begin a relationship with him if his true personality were known. The person lured into this relationship is flattered that someone would pay such singular attention to them because they, too, are starved for a sense of self. Many clients will tell me they remained oblivious to very obvious warning signs because they didn't want to lose the relationship.

Once these controlling partners are sure that they have "caught" a partner, they begin to act out their distorted beliefs. It is as though there is an emotional parasite in their soul that creates an insatiable appetite for attention and compliance with their will.

They are convinced they cannot live without their partner. In order to preserve the relationship, they begin to isolate their mate first from work, then from friends and finally from family. In order to know if their partner has gone anywhere other than where they said they were going, the "captor" will time their errands. When the hostage-partner says or does something that signals a possible move towards independence, the controlling partner, seized by the fear that they cannot survive without the other person, steps up their efforts to intimidate them.

If we are bleeding from a vein or artery, we know unless we stop the bleeding we will die. When possessive personalities sense their partner is leaving them, bleeding from them, they feel as though they are dying. This is why we hear the person say, "If I can't have you then no one will." What they are really saying is "Why should I let you leave so I can die?" By "having" their partner in death, they "have" them eternally.

You might be saying, "Aw, this is just a bunch of psychobabble. These people are just ticked off because they got jilted." Yes, it is true they are "ticked off" but they are angry because they are afraid. Anger grows out of fear of loss. Most of us understand that although it is painful to lose a partner, we will eventually pull ourselves together and go on. But controlling personalities are so devoid of personal resources that they cannot cope with being alone.

Jealous people are too undernourished spiritually and emotionally to be in partnership successfully. While everyone experiences twinges of jealousy at times, people who are perpetually jealous suffer from the, "Not Enough" syndrome. Their fundamental understanding of love is that there is only enough for one person. If mom loves you, she cannot love me, too. If my husband or wife has outside interests and friends, then he or she will not have time for me. The outside person who is perceived to be "getting" this "limited" love is the object of deep jealousy. In turn, the spouse who is trying to have a life in addition to a marriage feels frustrated and victimized. The result is an emotional Net Zero for both the possessor and the possessed.

A classic example of this occurs in blended families and spreads like cancer throughout the family system. Intellectually stepmom understands that dad loves his children from his first marriage, but can't stand it when he chooses their needs over hers. To her, it is a slight and a commentary on her "place" in the family, "proof" that he doesn't really love her. Humiliated that she takes a back seat to the kids, she becomes increasingly jealous of the children and angry with him. The more shrill she becomes, demanding that he put her first, the more he protects his children from her as he takes emotional shelter in his relationship with them. She now displays full-blown resentment for the children for knocking her out of first place and is indignant that he defends them. Conversely, he feels she is asking him to ignore the kids. Her jealousy infects him and he begins to engage in a complementary type of "Not Enough" thinking. He is afraid that if he loves his children, he will lose her, and if he loves her, he will lose the children. At her deepest level, she fears abandonment, because he will "use up" all his love on the children and have none left for her. The children absolutely understand this dynamic and become wary of both. Everyone is losing and no one is winning.

Another example of the "Not Enough" syndrome are partners who resent it when their spouses visit family or go out with friends. Of course, there are cases where there actually is a problem and the offending partner truly is spending too much time with other people, but most often, the partner fears she is not desirable enough to keep her spouse if he doesn't want to spend every minute with her.

The Myth of Self-Esteem feeds our fear that we are not good enough. This fear begets jealousy, which begets more fear. The opposite dynamic is true. The more love there is in your life, the more you have to give.

Jealousy contracts because when there is a shortage people begin to hoard. Love expands us spiritually, emotionally and psychologically.

Jealousy makes our world smaller and more threatening. Love broadens our world and opens our spirit to the richness of the universe.

Jealousy drives away those who want to love us and alienates the very people who would enrich and enlarge our life. Love draws people to us.

Jealousy makes the world a frightening place, emotional loss lurking behind every relationship. Love attracts others to the kindness that has taken up residence in our souls, deepening our connection to all humankind.

Jealousy makes every commitment tenuous. Love allows us to experience the exhilaration of committing to another. We learn to be miserly and hold a grudge when we are jealous. We learn to be generous and forgiving when we love. Love brings vulnerability and exposure to hurt but that is because love dismantles the defensiveness that jealousy builds.

When children have been deprived of love during formative stages of development, their experience of love teaches them that it is a limited commodity and the chances of running out of love loom large. It is virtually impossible for them to understand the expansive quality of love because their only experience of it is its absence. One cannot fully know the positive scope of something by experiencing its negative.

Early formation is so critical that a child who has been deprived of the basics essential to personality development such as trust, security, hope and a sense of place within a family face an uphill (and sometimes hopeless) battle to assimilate these fundamentals into their personality. Children deprived of food cannot shake the compulsion to eat as often as they can. They often hoard food even when there is ample food available. Children who are neglected, even benignly, can struggle for a lifetime to believe that someone could actually love them.

The ideal in relationship is to maintain one's self while remaining open to another. The Myth of Self Esteem leads us to think that everyone else is in love and that being in a relationship, at any cost, is more important than the destruction of one's self concept. "I don't know what's happened to me. . . . I've lost the person I used to be," is one of the most common complaints I hear from people about what's happened to them in their relationship. Loss of self is the erosion of those elements that comprise one's personality, one's unique self. Bit by bit a person's makeup is revised to suit the partner. This happens in healthy and loving relationships as well as destructive ones. In fact, the better the relationship the more difficult it is to recognize when this happens.

While changes can and should be expected as one makes the inevitable adjustment to being in relationship, burying the core self is deadly. As the core disappears, the sense of self is weakened, highlighting dependence on the partner and increasing the fear of being rejected. The person "hears" the message that her partner doesn't like some aspect of her. This message can be anything from a subtle gesture like eye rolling, a sigh, a veiled look of disdain or an outright criticism.

Rather than taking a step back to examine the dynamics of the message, the person responds in knee-jerk fashion and begins to modify not only behavior but her thought process as well. At a deep level, the psyche weighs the preservation of itself against losing the partner and chooses to please rather than preserve. This decision, conscious or unconscious, to become someone you are not is a fundamental betrayal of yourself. You are allowing another person's self-serving (and sometimes selfish) opinion to push your soul aside. You are allowing another person to unilaterally decide you are not okay.

Each time we hear a message from someone about ourselves, we need to evaluate. Does this message have merit or does this person have a hidden agenda? Are they attempting to manipulate us to suit an unreasonable need or are they authentically describing our behavior and its injurious effect on them? If we determine that they are, in fact, troubled by our behavior or views, what does that mean to us? Is there a voice within that tells us that our behavior needs to be changed or do we see that this is their problem? If a person cannot accept criticism, ever, and is hurt no matter what is said, then it is their problem. If, however, you blame and use sarcasm, then it is your problem. Only after being very honest with yourself should you make a judgment as to what behavior needs to be modified and what is justified.

Loss of self occurs when you stop pursuing something that you enjoy because someone else doesn't want you to do it. (This obviously doesn't apply if you pursue your interests selfishly, without regard to others' time and interests.) For instance, you enjoy antique shopping or model train shows but your partner complains about watching the kids while you're gone. You lose a piece of yourself when you decide not to go because it's easier than going through the hassle. Or, you begin to hide facets of your personality because your partner doesn't like them. If you have always been outgoing but because your partner says, "Do you have to talk to everyone you meet?" you begin to withdraw at social gatherings, then you are agreeing that who you are is defective.

Fear of loss is foundational to the Myth of Self-Esteem because instead of your self concept being built on internal approval, it is built on external approval. External approval is a powerful influence in the decision to enter into a relationship. If your self is built upon the approval of others, then being alone deprives you of approval.

Even if you are healthy and are not looking for someone to fill in the empty places, it is especially hard, whether by choice or circumstance, not to be in a relationship. While it is true that the majority of people are with someone, the fact is that for some, a relationship is either not desirable or available. The struggle to maintain a sense of your own integrity as a single in this culture is difficult at best. At family gatherings you may hear, "Still single?" or "Are you dating anyone yet?" the implication being that your life doesn't really begin until you are part of a couple. People who go out alone are viewed with pity by others. "Poor Rachel—she just can't seem to find anyone." Even the strongest of people admit that they cannot go into a restaurant and sit alone at a table. It is uncomfortable for them and for others sitting nearby. Rarely are they given a good seat; more often they are seated in a corner or close to the kitchen. The "good" seats are reserved for couples and families.

Being in a relationship is not a measure of your worth. Respecting and liking yourself, accepting your uniqueness as well as your faults and extending the same acceptance and understanding to others is honoring everyone's uniqueness and worth. This enriches not only yourself, but all humankind and confirms your "place" in the order of the universe. Respecting yourself and others is the basis of loving and being loved. It is the ultimate realization of God's purpose for us on earth.

# 9

# Work as Journey

*And only the Master shall praise us, and only the
Master shall blame; And no one shall work for
money, and no one shall work for fame; But each
for the joy of the working, and each, in his separate
star, Shall draw the Thing as he sees It, for the God
of Things as They Are!*—Rudyard Kipling, *The Seven
Seas: L'Envoi*

*I long to accomplish a great and noble task. But it
is my chief duty to accomplish small tasks as if
they were great and noble.*—Helen Keller

Work. Work is a loaded word. In Genesis, when God punishes Adam
and Eve for eating of the fruit of knowledge, God tells Adam that for
his disobedience, henceforth "by the sweat of your face you shall
eat your bread." Genesis 3:19a. Since that time, work has continued to be both a curse and a blessing. For those who do not find
their life's work it is a curse. For those who find themselves in their
life's work, it is a blessing. Obviously, everyone doesn't love their
job and to a certain degree, this will always be part of the human
condition. So, if we don't always have a big, fat choice in what we
do, why does work matter? It matters because work is the whole

nut. It is the barometer and the thermometer of who we are. It is the peephole into our soul and sometimes it is our soul. Work becomes what we interpret it to be and if we believe the Myth of Self-Esteem, then we believe that *what* we do is a measure of who we are. Work becomes the yardstick with which we compare ourselves to others. Are we making as much as Ralph? Are we as important as Mary?

Sometimes we denigrate ourselves based on how we view work. The Myth whispers in our ear that there is no dignity in certain jobs. Years ago, if someone's father was a clerk in a store, or delivered milk, it was considered respectable. Now these would be considered dead-end jobs. Our culture is so elitist that the intrinsic dignity in a job well done has been lost on several generations. We hear so often that it is hard to find good help, people who are dependable and take pride in their work. This is due, in part, to the lack of respect for work that does not pay well or is not high-status job. It is no wonder that people in low paying, low status employment do not take pride in a job well done because they do not feel respected and, as a consequence, do not respect themselves. America's numbing view of self-esteem warns that we must be successful and ever upwardly mobile; it certainly does not reward those who are content where they are.

Have you had someone helping you who was knowledgeable, kind and patient, someone who obviously knew their job and loved doing it? Wasn't there is a sense of profound relief that you found someone who happily helped you, someone who was competent, who cared and who stuck with you until the job was done? A person like that can change the whole tenor of your day; the world doesn't feel like such a bad place after all; there *are* nice people. And who among us has not had the experience of interacting with someone who clearly did not like their work and was resentful of anyone who made them do it? Rudeness, poor workmanship, incompetence, apathy, sloppy work—these are symptoms that emerge when the dignity of work is not acknowledged. This lack of nobility is symptomatic of the "Bigger Is Better" school of thought. Judging the relative importance of another human being based on their job is demeaning and arrogant. It shows the worst kind of spineless adherence to a hierarchy built on unhealthy pride.

There is a profound difference between failing to achieve a goal you have set for yourself and failing to achieve an artificial societal goal in order to look good to others. In the first case you are growing into your potential by challenging yourself and while you may not realize your final goal, at the deepest level, there is satisfaction in trying. There is no failure where someone has tried. In the second case, the person is a failure both in society's eyes and their own.

We may choose to simply pass time in our jobs—life starts when work is over—or we may decide to give ourselves fully to our work and let its own meaning emerge for us. In *Care of the Soul,* Thomas Moore discusses the concept of work as a "vocation, a calling from a place that is the source of meaning and identity . . ." [22] "But being a waitress is not the source of meaning and identity," you say. This may be so for you, but it doesn't mean that you can't accept the dignity of the work you are doing at the time. You can cultivate those qualities in yourself that are needed in that particular job and use them as you make your way through life.

People who are unhappy in their work are usually battling other demons in their lives. Their inability to find another job may be from a lack of self-respect or belief in their natural ability. Or they may be stuck in an unhealthy career because they are afraid of losing their status, income, or insurance.

Negative self-messages prevent you from assimilating the wisdom and rewards your work could bring. Moore reiterates this when he says, "Our work takes on narcissistic qualities when it does not serve well as a reflection of self. When that inherent reflection is lost, we become more concerned instead with how our work reflects on our reputations. We are tempted to find satisfaction in secondary rewards, such as money, prestige, and the trappings of success."[23]

The questions then, are: How do I see myself and is that reflection true to whom I am meant to be? Have I been influenced by the need to feel important or successful?

One of the saddest reflections of this attitude was a comment I overheard, directed to a high school senior with a 4.3 average who had decided to go into teaching. The parent said, "You're never going to make any money that way. Don't waste yourself teaching. Let someone who is not as smart as you do it." This is the Myth in all its cruel and damaging glory: *You are not important unless you are famous or rich.*

And what about the 2.0 student who struggled and studied hard and finally was able to graduate, one of the first in the family? This person might be very proud to be a produce manager.

The important piece of this is the question, *"How do you feel about yourself?"* If that produce manager values herself and her accomplishments, she is miles ahead of the executive vice president who feels shamed because his wasn't given better stock options with his last promotion.

Another work myth is the idea that until you are doing your "life work" you are wasting time. If you believe this it is because we, as a culture, have taught you to be impatient with the process of becoming. This time it is the McDonald's school of thought whereby everything is predictable and fast. Everyone should have the following statement in front of them at all times: *"Every step of the journey is the Journey,"* author unknown. This means nothing is a mistake or a waste and there are no absolutes, no guarantees. There is only every day with all that a day can bring. There is only the journey.

Theologically speaking, the ability to coexist with uncertainty is referred to as "living the question." This means that not only do we accept that life is not neat and predictable, but that it is in the unknown and unpredictable that the great truths dwell. When we live the question, we are submitting to Uncertainty, which ultimately will enrich us. Just as an airplane sometimes has to go from Washington, D.C., to Atlanta before it can go to Chicago, so, too, do our lives take indirect routes. Every moment of our pilgrimage holds meaning and purpose if we will look for it and claim it.

Each of us is essential to the universe and must fulfill our purpose. Elie Wiesel knows the horror of being a young boy in the concentration camps, of torture, of losing his family. I'm sure as a young boy he never dreamed of the impact his life would have. Yet he has also told us of the value of his experiences. His books reveal truths we could never know on our own. The same is true for Maya Angelou. Despite the abuse she endured, she reached into that wounded place and extracted truth. Weisel and Angelou and others like them challenge us to experience the world differently and view people through clear, unacculturated, lenses. They help us to view ourselves deeply, but with grace, so that we may extend it to others.

Each job we have, despite the loathing we may have for it, will present us with knowledge that is powerful and liberating. This is true even for those who are trapped in their job and feel neither powerful nor free. We can be sucked dry by our job or we can nourished by it. The difference is in how we view ourselves. Do you measure yourself negatively against others or do you reflect on where you are and how it is impacting your life?

One summer I worked in a factory on an assembly line, filling boxes with sewing patterns. I knew that for me it was only a summer job, but for many of the others, this was their job for the rest of their lives. As time went on, I noticed there were people who joked and laughed and generally used work as a backdrop for socializing, managing to ignore the monotony of their day. I also noticed that they usually had hobbies, projects or causes to which they devoted themselves outside of work.

Others kept their heads down and did their job, and still others complained loud and long about everything. For those who did their work silently or those who complained endlessly, it was evident that they believed they were powerless. They saw themselves as trapped and, being trapped, they couldn't imagine that their position could be positive and hopeful. It is unfortunate because all of them had the same basic internal resources available to redefine their lives.

If you can hold in your heart the awareness that each work experience can teach you a new truth, the easier it will be to understand the roadmap for your life; each time you change direction, your path will become clearer.

There will be those moments, however, when you do feel trapped or feel like you've made an unsalvageable mistake; when this feeling comes over you, remain open to this moment and don't give in to anxiety or negative thoughts. Daniel Goleman, in his book, *Emotional Intelligence,* describes the effects of anxiety on the brain's ability to produce effective thought.

> "Anxiety undermines the intellect . . .and is an almost sure predictor that a person will eventually fail. . . . When people who are prone to worry are asked to perform a cognitive task . . .it is the negative thoughts . . . that are found to most directly disrupt their decision-making."[24]

Have you ever been in a hurry, or so panicky that you can't remember someone's name or a phone number you've used a thousand times? This is similar to the mental block you experience if you think you are trapped or have made an irretrievable mistake. To reverse this self-destructive thinking, yield to what you are meant to learn from this experience. As you practice this course of thought, you will quickly begin to see possibilities and will stop from worrying about your performance, choices or circumstance.

Breaking the Myth's hold on you means to fully partake of your own life as it unfolds. Being at peace doesn't mean you are free of struggles or doubts. These are components of a real life, not weaknesses or failures. When you find yourself in a funk, recognize that your soul is warning that a change is necessary.

Meaningful work is not always available; further, work that is meaningful *to us* is not always valued by our culture. We can be liberated from the tyranny of what culture approves and disapproves of by staying focused on the meaningfulness of our work and by choosing how we allow it to influence our journey.

It might seem as though we wouldn't experience any problems if our work were successful or culturally endorsed, but jobs or careers that pay well *at the expense of others* eventually inflict a mortal wound. The movie *Wall Street* is an example of how a mortal wound occurs. In the movie, a young stockbroker desperately wants to be as successful as his boss and in an effort to boost his standing with him, the neophyte ends up selling out his own father. Although this is a story about people who make more money in one year than some of us will make in a lifetime, it illustrates the treacherous results of success gone bad.

One of my college roommates landed a great job after she graduated. She had an expense account, excellent health benefits, a company car and the freedom to schedule her own time, an ideal job. Even though her husband was also well paid, the expense of living in a large city meant her salary was critical. Despite trying to ignore it, she was haunted by working for a tobacco company. While she had once smoked herself, she had come to the conclusion that not only was smoking harmful but that to participate in the distribution of cigarettes was morally wrong.

Realistically, she realized that quitting the job wasn't going to bring the tobacco companies to their knees. Someone else would just replace her and she would be out of a job. Despite her convictions, she continued in the job. Finally, disturbed by violating her own ethical code, she decided that no matter how much she needed the income and how successful she was, for her, it was not success. She quit despite frantic pleadings from her family that jobs like this don't come around every day and she would be sorry. She never really was.

Our work, whether we like our particular job or not, is one of the principal elements of our pilgrimage to wholeness. We are tempted to judge ourselves by our work (or lack of it) because, fueled by the Myth, society judges us that way. If we allow ourselves to listen this Myth, as Jason's Argonauts listened to the sirens, we will perish on the rocks of self-hatred.

There is one more aspect of work that cannot be forgotten; it is the flip side of being an employee—being an employer. Much of our illness, physical and emotional in the workplace today, can be traced to corporate worship at the feet of Profit. This has produced some of the worst greed in our history—greed which has cost lives and shattered families. The list is endless. An automobile company that refuses to recall cars with exploding gas tanks because it would cost too much. Cigarettes made more addictive with additives. Surplus baby formula sold to countries with contaminated water supplies. Toxic waste disposed of in water sources. Unsafe factory conditions— asbestos, chemicals, locked escape doors. Denying necessary medical procedures to save the HMO money.

What these examples all have in common is the desire to make money at any cost. Money means power. Successful CEOs are written up in trade magazines, touted as geniuses, admired and emulated. But when you peel back the cosmetic victory, it repeatedly exposes a person who downsized thousands of employees just before Christmas or played a shell game with profits and losses. And when does the buck stop? It stops when someone who matters finally suffers a loss. Healthcare, was not an issue for a particular congressman until he discovered his daughter's illness was not covered under his health plan. An honest man, he admits he was humbled by his experience and now crusades, not only for universal health coverage but for loophole-free benefits.

If greedy and sociopathic corporate players cared that their soul was stained with the blood and tears of their victims, we would not have tragedy after tragedy in the workplace. If our culture valued people over profits, then CEOs or top government officials would not be worried about their prestige or reputation. They would be free to run their companies or agencies with integrity and responsibility for both employees and consumers. Naïve, you say? Maybe. But what would happen if prestige and wealth was NOT a measure of personal worth? Postal workers would never have spawned the phrase, "going postal," factory employees would be alive, seniors would retire with their full pensions. We would be a nation of integrity where wealth and prestige are not as central as the uniqueness and importance of each person. Just as stranger helping stranger spread like wildfire across the nation after September 11, so could integrity become the hallmark of America.

# 10

# Rest as Ritual

*Rest, rest, perturbed spirit!*
*Hamlet I, 5,* —Shakespeare

On the average, we Americans work longer hours and more days per week than our counterparts in other first world countries We work, on the average, 9.2 hours per day. Thirty-three percent of Americans work on the weekend.[25] You would think with this work record, we would take more time off, or at least take more quality time off. But we don't. The average American income is about the same as the average income of sixty-five other nations; however, the average Swede gets five to eight weeks of paid vacation per year, the French and Germans get six weeks and the average American gets thirteen days with thirty-five percent reporting they get less than ten days per year.[26] In the fifties, people thought that all the timesaving devices that were being developed would free up more time. Well, yes, they did free up more time . . . to work.

We work on our vacations, we work on the weekends, we work in the car, we work on planes. Thanks to computers and cell phones, we are no longer inaccessible in the mountains or on boats. Except for the Japanese who are more driven than we, Americans don't know what it means to rest. Rest, from the Latin, *restare* means to stop, stand, remain. Our idea of rest is to run faster and do more. Let's eavesdrop on a conversation between two co-workers.

"Hey, Ed, where'yu goin' for your vacation?"

"Nowhere," replies Ed somewhat furtively. "Jus' gonna stay home." Pause.

"Yeah—that's what I oughta do. Y' gonna catch up on all those projects around the house?"

"No. Jus' gonna lay around, relax."

The coworker turns and walks back to his work area "What a waste of a vacation," he mutters under his breath.

Oh, we would like to think we are more enlightened than that. We know we run around too much but think that with meditation, Yoga and relaxation exercises we are taking care of ourselves. We would be . . . if we actually did these things.

Let's take a look at the typical nine-day American vacation which begins Friday night and ends the following Sunday. Friday we find the Smiths taking off early from work to finish getting ready—laundry, packing, taking care of last-minute details. Saturday morning, early, they finish loading the car and get on the road, traveling most of the day. They arrive at vacation destination in time for 3:00 check in. They unload the car and throw their stuff in the room before taking off for the remainder of the day, determined to use every bit of vacation time. The next six days consist of being at designated places at designated times in order to catch shows or tours, or beat the crowds. There are always crowds. For six to eight hours a day the Smiths might cycle, rock climb, hike, scuba dive, shop or stand in line at the amusement park. Oh, there may be some beach sitting and an occasional nap but generally, the Smiths will go from morning until night in pursuit of getting the most out of the six days they have. They will also engage in the greatest vacation activity of all, consuming vast amounts of the basic food groups: Fat, sugar, starch, caffeine, chocolate and alcohol.

Checkout time is Saturday, 10:00 A.M., which means the Smiths get up, throw things back in the suitcase, jump in the car to head back, wait in long lines of traffic or for delayed flights with all the other vacationers who had to check out on Saturday. When they finally arrive at home either Saturday or Sunday, our exhausted friends spend the remaining time unpacking, washing clothes and putting things away . . . or not. Some, honing their avoidance technique to razor-sharp precision, plop in front of the computer or TV. The next morning, in their T-shirts and shorts, they tiptoe out to the car where they fish their suitcase out from under the mound of stuff that self-generates in a car in the course of a vacation. Exhausted and decidedly unenthusiastic, they drag in to work, successful yet again in defeating the purpose of a vacation.

While for some, this may be a somewhat exaggerated depiction of Americans at leisure, the sad fact is that it is very close to the truth. If only our Pilgrim forefathers and mothers could see us now. They would be proud that there isn't a wasted moment to provide idle hands for the devil's workshop.

Our weekdays are even worse. We all know the script: carpools, long days at work, commuting, chores, children's activities, church and community meetings. Weekends are even more packed.

Why don't we know how to rest? Why can't we get up and have nothing to do the whole day?

We think that we are not really living unless we are sampling everything life has to offer. We are afraid that if we don't, everyone else will be more fulfilled, have a better time than we. If our kids aren't doing the same we feel guilty because they might fall behind other kids who are busy achieving, achieving, achieving.

The Myth of Self-Esteem has convinced us that *doing* is more important than *being*. That doing is a measure of success—success at being successful, success at generating leisure "results," such as pictures of us *doing*, with souvenirs, tans and newly learned skills as proof. It would be boring, I admit, to have an album bursting with pictures of people reading books or swinging in a hammock.

People thinking. Pictures of people doing nothing. The closest we come to doing nothing is watching movies or renting videos.

We are a country suffering from emotional insomnia, our minds fuzzy from sleep deprivation, mental exhaustion, a lack of balance in our lives and a lack of renewal. We simply don't know how to rest. What constitutes rest is highly individualistic but like Justice Potter Stuart once said about pornography, "I can't define it but I'll know it when I see it." Rest is like that—it is hard to define but most people know what rest is for them.

At the very least, rest would free your mind to wander. Rest would not place stress upon you. Rest would leave you feeling refreshed, renewed. It would reconnect you to yourself. If you were rested, you would not feel overwhelmed by your problems and you would feel that there are ways to deal with them. Genuine rest leaves you feeling hopeful and ready to begin again.

What rest is for one person may be work to another. Some feel rested by fishing, others by sitting on the beach looking at the ocean, still others by camping or hiking. There is a thin line between engaging in an activity that frees the mind and an activity which constrains it. People who do things like mountain climbing claim they feel great . . . and they may. They may feel invigorated, renewed and accomplished, but I would argue that they are not rested. Climbing puts a person under tremendous mental and physical strain. The climber is in a perpetual state of danger which means the adrenaline is pumping and the heart is racing. In many respects, this is the antithesis of rest.

On the other hand, gardening can be relaxing and soul renewing even though there may be a physical challenge. One is outside, connecting with the promise that the natural world provides, a perpetual sense of nature's resurrection. Plants grow, plants die, new plants take their place. Working in the soil is the experience of life at its most basic and hope at its most cosmic.

People who garden are not getting an adrenaline rush. They are not under intense mental or physical strain, even though there may be a physical expenditure of energy, lifting trees or shoveling dirt. The difference between gardening and mountain climbing is danger, mental and physical strain, intensity, and life or death concentration.

Although Dr. Herbert Benson and his book, *Timeless Healing,* will be discussed later in this chapter, it is important to note here that in an effort to induce what he calls the relaxation response, Dr. Benson states:

"Sitting or standing, walking or swimming, even knitting and crocheting, is the repetitive quality of the exercise that helps engender the relaxation response. In the same way a parent can be assured of a few moments of rest by putting a baby in an automatic swing, the brain and the body can take advantage of the rest inherent in an easy, repetitive task, creating a kind of hypnotic effect.[27]

Meditation is the purest form of conscious rest and is the best method to achieve quietude. It is a challenge to sit quietly when, within seconds, our minds keep returning to the Thought Olympics, racing from one idea to another. Meditation restores perspective and balance in our lives and provides a deeper peace than activity-driven rest; five minutes of meditation can be the equivalent of a day of relaxation.

Meditation is not as mysterious and time consuming as you may think. Even though you may have a hard time sitting and doing nothing (or *especially* if you have a hard time sitting and doing nothing), it is worth cultivating. In his book, *Wherever You Go, There You Are: Mindfulness Meditation in Everyday Life,* Jon Kabat-Zinn does a nice job of explaining meditation, making it approachable and feasible. If you keep at it, over time your mind will quiet and you will begin to experience the sense of peace that comes with surrendering your mind.

Creativity is another facet of rest. Lost time—timelessness during creativity—as discussed in chapter six, applies here. Creativity releases the mind from repetitive thought patterns allowing it to enter a level of consciousness that rejuvenates and restores. Sleep, meditation and creativity all do essentially the same thing: they create brain waves that release the mind from negative or tiring activity.

When we don't rest, we lose our perspective. We are blinded to what is important because we are focused on the mundane. When we step back and allow our minds and bodies to rest, our thoughts slow down, our breathing deepens and our muscles relax. These motor responses are physical metaphors for emotional and spiritual release.

Letting go is the foundation of Eastern philosophy. By not hanging on to what we think we want, we experience authentic freedom. The *Tao Te Ching,* a book believed to be written around 500 B.C., embodies this fundamental Chinese principle of allowing life to flow around you. This lesson from the *Tao* is illustrative of this idea:

> Fill your bowl to the brim
> and it will spill.
> Keep sharpening your knife
> And it will be blunt.
> Chase after money and security
> And your heart will never  unclench
> Care about people's approval
> And your will be their prisoner.
> Do your work, then step back.
> The only path to serenity.[28]

Serenity is the state of being balanced and in harmony, not only with what is right and good, but also with what is. This perspective is possible if we allow ourselves to experience the world *as it exists* within the natural and cosmic flow of events. Our choice is to struggle against or accept this cosmic flow. Another way to say this is that we can choose to accept or reject God's will for us.

Acceptance is misunderstood in Western thinking. We tend to

think of acceptance as giving in, becoming powerless. In fact, acceptance allows us to focus on what needs to be done rather than attacking a problem by throwing everything we have at it in an attempt to prevail.

In The *Seven Spiritual Laws of Success*, Deepak Chopra cites The Law of Least Effort, or Acceptance as the Fourth Spiritual Law, explaining that we must acknowledge the situation exactly as it is in the present moment rather than as we wish it would be.[29] This does not mean that we have to *like* the situation; it simply means that in order to act, we must have factual starting point. When I talk about this concept, inevitably someone will say to me, "You mean I'm supposed to 'accept' that fact that someone has just attacked me in the parking lot? I'm supposed to do nothing?"

Quite the contrary. If you think, "I can't believe this is happening to me," you lose crucial reaction time wishing something wasn't happening. If you practice acceptance you would think "I'm being attacked . . . I have to do something." While this is an exaggerated example, and most people who have faced this situation would not be able to break down their reactions in such a contrived manner, it is still illustrative of the process.

Researchers have pinpointed the reason a calm, studied approach actually allows our brain to work at its optimum. Daniel Goleman explains this process in his book, *Emotional IQ:*

> "The connections between the amygdala and the neocortex . . . explains why emotion is so crucial to effective thought, both in making wise decisions and in simply allowing us to think clearly. . . . circuits from the limbic brain to the prefrontal lobes mean that the signals of strong emotion—anxiety, anger and the like—can create neural static, sabotaging the ability of the prefrontal lobe to maintain working memory. That is why when we are emotionally upset we say we 'just can't think straight.' "[30]

In other words, by remaining calm, we are better able to correctly assess our situation and more likely to act appropriately than if we are angry, upset or hurt. This is just another way of saying the same thing as the *Tao* when it says, "We work with being, but non-being is what we use."[31]

This concept of acceptance is also vital to our health. Mentioned earlier with respect to relaxation, Dr. Herbert Benson also addresses this issue from the viewpoint of serenity. Dr. Benson has been part of the pioneering effort to understand the exact connection between body and mind. His book, *Timeless Healing,* details the technique he developed called the Relaxation Response whereby patients learn relaxation techniques (coupled with other healing methods) which enable them to experience natural healing when anxiety is sabotaging their health. Although researching from a medical perspective, Dr. Benson's findings ultimately agree with the work of Daniel Goleman regarding the presence of anxiety and emotion as it affects decision-making. Dr. Benson states:

> "The relaxation response nullifies, to a certain extent, the action of noradrenaline, so that the body does not react as radically to mildly stressful events but retains the ability to respond immediately to major threats. . . . For all patients, the relaxation response is not only a short-term boon but a long-term balm."[32]

Goleman and Benson both believe that our thoughts, perceptions and reactions directly affect the actual physiology of our mind. If we cannot cultivate a non-anxious self-presence—serenity—life will be one long struggle. Achieving serenity requires that we turn deaf ears to the Myth of Self-Esteem that disdains our attempts to care for ourselves (John Wayne again). The Myth encourages us, instead, to sacrifice our emotional and spiritual needs to the insatiable gods of pride, competition and productivity.

You know better than anyone what you need. In the midst of your ordinary life, your internal voice, your soul, warns you of what you need. While it would be nice to take a month off, the reality is that most of us cannot. However, you can eliminate those factors in your life that rob you of your vitality. You can refuse those activities that leave you no time for yourself. You can meditate and learn to relax. You can resist the mind-set of the Myth, which arrogantly asserts that it is wasteful to do nothing. Contrary to what it may feel like, these down times can give you back to yourself. It is these periods of simple being that allow you to connect to the spiritual. "Being" is rooted in the idea of being owned by nothing, owing nothing. Lao-tzu describes the importance of being thusly:

> "We join spokes together in a wheel,
>
> But it is the center hole
>
> That makes the wagon move.
>
> We shape clay into a pot,
>
> But it is the emptiness inside
>
> That holds whatever we want.
>
> We hammer wood for a house,
>
> But it is the inner space that makes it livable.
>
> We work with being,
>
> But non-being is what we use."[33]

# 11

# Damning with Faint Praise

*Praising all alike, is praising none.*—John Gay,
"Epistle to a Lady"

Our culture has a problem with overpraising children. Perhaps Dr. Spock had a lot to do with it. Perhaps the sixties had something to do with it. Perhaps Women's Liberation contributed. Maybe they all did with the result that for the past thirty years or so almost everything children do is praised.

Excessive praise certainly didn't exist when I was a kid. For most of us born before the sixties, praise from our teachers, coaches and parents was sparse; but, when we did hear it, we knew we had done something pretty darn good. It was a sign our accomplishment stood out. In other words, we knew we had earned it fair and square.

Somewhere along the line all that changed. Children's accomplishments moved to center stage and were praised. And praised and praised (clapping is integral). Everybody is happy, happy, happy that little Will put his toy in the box. Grownups stop what they're doing to praise Will, even grown-ups who don't know little Will.

We have morphed into a culture that has become so child-centered that there are now families who impose little or no discipline, believing it will damage their children's self-esteem. These parents, some of whom are children who were overpraised themselves, became parents with shaky self-concepts who are now afraid of their own kids. Television reality shows, like "Super Nanny" and "Nanny 911", have emerged to help these adults deal with the thirty-pound gorillas they have, in turn, created. These parents aren't stupid; they are good people who are simply exhausted by children who understand (correctly) that *they*, not the parents, are in charge.

Despite displays to the contrary, children don't want to be in charge. It scares them to be in charge. They want parents who are in charge because they know they're not old enough to be in charge. They want their parents to be strong because it makes them feel secure. Parents who are unsure about disciplining, who give vapid praise, who allow children to speak disrespectfully to them, produce children who are unsure of themselves.

Children are unsure because their little inner voice is telling them that what they are doing is wrong, but when they look up and see that Dad going to pretend it didn't happen and isn't going to do anything about it, they're confused. And disappointed. Mom is a pushover. Dad's pretending nothing happened. Who's going to make me stop? This is scary. Even I know I shouldn't be in charge. Maybe if I scream a bad word at her she'd do something. "I hate you!" Mom looks angry, but she still isn't doing anything. She wouldn't let me do these bad things if it mattered. I can probably do whatever I want and she wouldn't care. I must not be important enough to matter. If I did matter, they would love me. It doesn't matter so they must not love me.

At one time I worked with adolescents in a psychiatric hospital and many of these kids had serious suicide attempts under their belts. Their depression was most often expressed as anger, but I was surprised when I discovered what they were really angry about. They weren't angry about parents who wouldn't get off their back.

They weren't angry about parents who made them keep their curfew. No, they were angry because they had parents who didn't care about them. I heard about parents who were too involved with a new spouse to spend time with them or who didn't check up on where they were or who forgot to pick them up. One boy with piercings and black fingernail polish broke down and sobbed, saying he just wanted his mother to know who he was; a mother who would spend some time with him.

Yes, these were deeply troubled children, a small percentage of the total adolescent population, but whether a parent actually neglects a child or benignly neglects them by letting them do what they want, the message is the same: A parent who doesn't care sends the single-most devastating message a child can receive and it has long-term ramifications.

This is not a blanket condemnation of an entire generation. These examples illustrate the creeping power that the Myth of Self-Esteem has over us. When we believe that negative feedback or discipline ruins a child's self-worth, the whole point of positive self-development has been lost.

So, while it is true that a classroom reward jar is a lot more appealing than a rap across the knuckles by Sister Marita Louise, there is something to be said about hard-earned praise.

Positive self-development is built upon success. However, when actions are artificially or overpraised, one of two things happens. The person either believes that they are, indeed, fabulous or instinctively knowing that the praise is unmerited, they feel ashamed and complicit. If this happens enough, a person's self-concept becomes distorted

In an eye-opening study William B. Swann, a professor at the University of Texas at Austin, found that when people had a choice of who would evaluate them, those with low self-esteem more often chose a negative evaluator over a positive one. Swann also found that people with low self-esteem felt closer to their partners when the partner judged them negatively, unlike those with higher self-esteem who felt closer to their spouses when they were evaluated positively.[34] These people are hurt by negative evaluations, but it is what they are most comfortable with. It is why people who are abused as children are more likely than those who were not abused to stay in an abusive relationship.

We should not fool ourselves into thinking our children don't catch on to undeserved praise until they're older. They understand at a tender age. I know. I have it on tape. It was Christmas morning and my five-year-old son had just received a plastic Viking helmet, sword and shield. The helmet was not cooperating and kept slipping over his eye despite repeated efforts to keep it looking, well, Vikingly. Sensing his frustration, I exclaimed that he looked quite fierce. He became visibly uncomfortable and said that he was not and I shouldn't say it because it wasn't true. He didn't like being praised for something that he had not earned or achieved. He just wanted the damn Viking helmet to stay on.

Ask someone about a favorite teacher or coach. The majority will probably say something to the effect that "she was the hardest teacher I ever had but boy do I know my grammar" or "he was a tough coach, but I had my best years under him." When you have worked hard for something, your pride in accomplishing it can never be taken away.

That part of my son that responded to me was his conscience which, thankfully, was pretty intact. Children wish to be rewarded for what they have genuinely achieved and instinctively know when that is the case. If children are overpraised, a funny thing happens. They begin to have less self-confidence rather than more.

In an article about praise, author Cassandra Vermillion says, "The problem with that kind of 'super, marvelous' praise is that . . . we don't believe it. In fact, it can even make us feel worse."[35] Overpraising kids is insidious. Here is, essentially, the process that goes on in a child's brain: "Number one, they are lying because they don't want to tell the truth. Number two, the truth is I'm not any good or they wouldn't have to lie." Over time children believe they are being praised for easy things because their parents don't think they are capable of doing better. Alfie Kohn in his article titled "Five Reasons to Stop Saying "Good Job!"[36] states, "In short, 'Good Job' doesn't reassure children; ultimately, it makes them feel less secure." To offset this feeling, children begin to "perform" to elicit more praise. But the assurance is short-lived and soon they are looking for something else to elicit praise. They forget what it is like to feel good based on their own sense of accomplishment and aren't sure if it's genuine when they do feel good. In short, they are dependent on praise to feel good.

A child who has been overpraised usually also feels shameful. Shame is feeling bad about who you are, guilt is feeling bad about something you did and embarrassment is when your transgressions become public. Shame is worse than guilt or embarrassment because when the person feels shame, he believes at his core he is incompetent or bad.

Praise is ineffectual when children are praised for something they should have done anyway. If it is Matthew's job to feed the dog, commending him for feeding the dog gives him the message that he is doing something extra, that you owe him something when he does it. Misdirected praise breaks down a sense of responsibility. What happens when Matthew doesn't feed the dog? Dad reminds him, maybe two or three times and then Matthew starts to complain that he's too busy or it's not fair. In a therapy session I had with a mother and her son, the mother pointed out that her son wouldn't put the peanut jar away when he was finished with it. In response, the boy actually said to the mother, "It's not my jar, it's yours. You bought it. You're the one who has to put it away." He was absolutely serious.

Whether it's doing household chores or pitching in at school, if a child doesn't feel she is a part of a larger universe, she will not feel significant and will be disconnected, selfish, lonely and angry.

There are a number of programs throughout the country that pair prison inmates with retired racehorses. Most of the inmates started with no experience but liked working with horses so much they put up with injuries and turned down other work opportunities to stay in the program. For many it was the first time they felt needed. One prisoner wanted to adopt his horse when he was released from prison. Another decided to go into ranching. These programs are rehabilitation not only for the horses but for the men as well. One inmate said that the experience changed him in an extraordinary way that he couldn't really explain. For some of these men, it was not only that the horses were completely dependent on them, but it was feeling connected that brought them out of their world of fear, anger and revenge.

What does this have to do with petulant children and teens? It has to do with feeling needed, feeling important in the grand scheme of things. For just about any kid, emptying the trash may not seem monumental, but it means he has an importance in the household. Being praised doesn't create this same sense of importance; it doesn't have weight and meaning the way responsibility does.

Kohn also points out that children tend to lose interest in a project when the praise stops. Here again, it is the praise that is the motivator, not the project or the accomplishment.

With overpraising, kids can become arrogant; after all, everything they do is seems pretty great. This arrogance unconsciously masks their insecurity and they may go on to become arrogant adults who believe they are better than anyone else and entitled to special treatment.

Not too long ago a restaurateur had to put a sign up reminding parents that if they did not keep their children under control, they would be asked to leave. Apparently the owner had asked the parents to keep their children from running around which is bad enough in itself. When that didn't work, he put up the sign. Predictably, some parents were offended that someone would point out that their children were making it difficult for others to enjoy the restaurant. Some parents didn't think their children were doing anything wrong; some felt entitled to be in a restaurant despite the disruptive behavior of their children. The other people in the restaurant didn't really didn't matter to them. What does this teach these children? It teaches them that they don't have to practice self-restraint.

Stories abound from friends who own businesses and have hired summer or after-school help. While there more great kids than not-so-great kids, it was the ones who felt entitled that drove the business owners nuts. Some of the behaviors were: Failing to show up for shifts and not only not calling but, incredibly, thinking nothing of not showing up and not calling; answering the store phone with a smart-aleck phrase, "Shoes," instead of "Murphy's Shoes, may I help you?"; standing behind the counter when other things needed to be done in the store. No customers, well, it wasn't their job to unpack merchandise or tidy up.

Can I prove that these kids were over praised? Of course not. The point is, this is the type of behavior overpraising can produce, someone who doesn't examine their behavior because they never had to growing up. Overpraising produces kids who don't think they have to put out much effort to get what they want; they truly do believe it should just be given to them. In effect, they become narcissists who think the world is there to serve them and meet their every desire.

A false sense of self-importance can cause some people, who believe they are superior, to keep score, diminishing others in order to assure themselves that they're better. We've all known people like this and most of us dislike them. People who keep score at work can be treacherous, especially if your work outshines theirs. Who hasn't heard of a boss who takes credit for an idea an employee had? And people who keep score in a relationship for their own sense of self-worth can be the end of the relationship.

Some of you may be saying to yourself, "I came from great parents who think the world of me . . . so why don't I have more self-confidence?" There are many reasons people don't feel good about themselves but those who come from a supportive home who are not confident may not know what it is like to feel the success they have earned. They may have been dependent on external validation to know whether or not they were successful. If you are dependent on someone else's opinion, you never really learn to trust your own experience. You may feel successful but if no one says anything . . . hmm . . . maybe you aren't successful.

It is imperative for a child to work at something and then have time to decide if he is successful or not. Kohn astutely points out that ,"Every time we say, 'Good Job!', . . . we're telling a child how to feel."[37] If you have worked hard and know it, having someone tell you that is great. But praise and recognition should never and can never substitute for the feeling you get from the achievement itself.

Why so much time on this? Because this is a book about the pitfalls of our distorted view of self-esteem and how to "get" it. Some of you may have been overpraised as children. Some of you may have fallen into the "Praise Trap" with your own children. It is not too late! The true gift of children is that they are quick to forgive and adjust well to the right kind of change: Warning, they will not like it at first.

The gift of true living is that every day is a chance for redemption. Every day we can learn from the day before. We are not condemned to failure; we can come to understand more about ourselves and formulate thinking that nurtures and heals us. Just because we have done it wrong the day before, and the day before that, doesn't mean we have to do it wrong today.

# 12

# The Pea under the Mattress

*There was once a prince, and he wanted a princess, but then she must be a real princess. He traveled right around the world to find one, but there was always something wrong. There were plenty of princesses, but whether they were real princesses he had great difficulty in discovering; there was always something which was not quite right about them. So at last he had come home again, and he was very sad because he wanted a real princess so badly.*

*One evening there was a terrible storm; it thundered and lightninged and the rain poured down in torrents; indeed it was a fearful night.*

*In the middle of the storm somebody knocked at the town gate, and the old king himself went to open it.*

*It was a princess who stood outside, but she was in a terrible state from the rain and the storm. The water streamed out of her hair and her clothes; it ran in at the top of her shoes and out at the heel, but she said that she was a real princess.*

*"Well we shall soon see if that is true," thought the old queen, but she said nothing. She went into the bedroom, took all the bed clothes off and laid a pea on the bedstead: then she took twenty*

*mattresses and piled them on top of the pea, and then twenty feather beds on top of the mattresses. This was where the princess was to sleep that night. In the morning they asked her how she slept.*

*"Oh, terribly bad!" said the princess. "I have hardly closed my eyes the whole night! Heaven knows what was in the bed. I seemed to be lying upon some hard thing, and my whole body is black and blue this morning. It is terrible!"*

*They saw at once that she must be a real princess when she had felt the pea through twenty mattresses and twenty feather beds. Nobody but a real princess could have such a delicate skin.*

*So the prince took her to be his wife, for now he was sure that he had found a real princess, and the pea was put into the museum, where it may still be seen if no one has stolen it.*

*Now this is a true story.*[38]

There are certain hidden behaviors that are seldom discussed but, nonetheless will erode your nobility and dishonor your Self. It may not be pleasant to hear some of these messages but if you are true royalty, like the princess who was bothered by the pea under the mattress, some of it may disturb you.

The nub, the heart, the foundation of this chapter is integrity. Integrity is the forgotten relative in the Myth of Self-Esteem. The Myth's emphasis on doing and succeeding doesn't leave a lot of room for integrity.

Integrity is not easy to define because it encompasses a number of philosophical ideas. For our purposes, let's just say that integrity is doing the right thing regardless of circumstances; it is upholding standards when it's not easy to do so; it is being trustworthy. Someone came up with a pretty good definition when they said, "Integrity is what you do when no one is looking."

Integrity can be a quiet and subtle quality . . . but it is the unconditional foundation of your character. In the fairy tale the prince finds that although there are lots of princesses, "there was always something which was not quite right about them." If you do not have integrity, there will always be something which is not quite right about you. Lack of principle will nibble at your soul until all that remains is the skeleton of your character. People can sense your lack of integrity and instinctively will not trust you. You will never really like yourself as long as a cloud of disingenuousness overshadows your accomplishments.

When you lack integrity, you cannot be authentic with God, with others or with yourself and you will drift further and further from the person you were intended to be. When you do not honor your sacredness, you teach others not to honor it either. In many places in the Bible, there are references to people who have compromised their integrity by hardening their hearts to the truths that they had learned. The more you act without principle, the easier it becomes to do it again and again and again until finally your heart hardens to whom you have become. You will lose the moral compass that even young children have. While children's integrity is somewhat selfish—their chief concern is not getting in trouble or making Mom and Dad angry—it nevertheless carries with it an innate knowledge of right and wrong.

There is little rational difference, however, between a child who does something wrong and an adult who has no integrity. Both are thinking only of the immediate moment, of whether or not they're going to get caught and neither is concerned with the overarching consequences of their behavior on themselves or others.

Daniel Goleman does a masterful job of describing the process of moving toward integrity in his book, *Emotional Intelligence* when he interprets the effects of impulse control on emotional maturity.[39] The Marshmallow Test, developed by Walter Mischel at Stanford, explores whether or not four-year-olds can resist their desire to eat a marshmallow while the researcher, who has been in the room with them, leaves to do some supposed errands. The children are told that they can either eat a marshmallow right away, or they can wait until the researcher comes back and then have two. Roughly one third of the children grabbed the one marshmallow right away while the other two-thirds distracted themselves in various ways so they could wait and receive the two-marshmallow reward.

The researchers tracked these children throughout their school years and discovered striking differences between the "grabbers" and the "waiters." The "grabbers" tended to be shy, stubborn, indecisive, easily upset, mistrustful, self doubting, prone to jealousy, and had a tendency, with their sharp temper, to get into fights and arguments. Their SAT scores were a whopping 210 points lower than the "waiters."

Goleman concludes that people who cannot control their impulses and who cannot postpone rewards are emotionally immature, regardless of their chronological age. Emotional maturity, which means having self-discipline, is the basis upon which integrity is built. Even if you have managed occasionally to escape the tentacles of the Self-Esteem Myth, if you disregard your character or minimize the importance of ethics, all the success and effort toward self-actualization will be wasted.

What are some of the behaviors that get in the way of integrity? What may surprise you is not the actions themselves, but their capacity to erode self-respect. Following are the predominant behaviors that will undermine your integrity:

### Lying

When you tell "little" lies in order to avoid taking responsibility for your conduct, to make yourself look better, or to claim credit where credit is not due, you are lying. Period.

Honesty is the underpinning of character and a person who lies does not adhere to even fundamental standards. When someone lies, they are creating a fraudulent premise and will need to engage in ever-expanding dishonest behavior in order to validate themselves. Lying erodes their spirit, leaving them with little self-respect since any success they have, they may have come by dishonestly like putting inflated information on a resumé. The

Myth of Self-Esteem is a factor in the propensity to lie because one's tendency is to lie rather than be wrong. It is far better to tell the truth, even if you are ashamed or feel foolish because life's best lessons are learned from *mistakes*. In fact, telling the truth when it is hard to do so only increases a person's respect for you.

## Gossiping

The need to gossip grows from an inner emptiness and a need to feel superior. When you know the latest or juiciest you are seen as an insider, someone significant enough to be told important or high level information. This is a sad waste of a person's energy. It is like being so immersed in soap operas that the characters become real.

When a person is busy and meaningfully engaged, gossip is unappealing and unproductive. People gossip in an attempt to gain stature like a newspaper reporter tries to get a scoop. These people live vicariously through someone else's dramas. They get an initial rush when they gossip, thus providing a buzz to a life that is boring and unfulfilling.

The excitement of gossip dissipates quickly and like an addictive drug, it drives the person to search for another fix . . . more gossip. When the person is alone, and if she is honest, she realizes that the damage she has done by gossiping, combined with the emptiness in her spirit, is debilitating. It strips her of what dignity she may have had before. Unfortunately, even though there may be moments of remorse, until the person decides to stop or at get help, it will happen again and again.

## Untrustworthiness and/or undependability

If a person can't be trusted or doesn't carry out the tasks he has been asked to do, he doesn't value others. Sooner or later every person has a problem finishing something. However, when it is a chronic problem, it is a character flaw because the person won't take corrective measures to become responsible.

Unreliability shows a deep lack of integrity; instead of doing the assigned task, the person is content not only to cause a mess, but also to stand by and watch others suffer as a result. It also introduces a hard-to-shake negativity into the relationship.

"Ken, my meeting is in five minutes. Where are the color-coded agendas?"

"Ah, well, I just haven't had time to get to them." Ken's boss must now go into the meeting empty-handed, embarrassed and fumbling for an explanation as to why he has no agenda. Ken cannot be trusted and both he and his boss know it.

### Sneakiness

Sneakiness is about lack of courage. It is the lack of courage to take responsibility for what one has done, hasn't done or wants to do. It is amazing how quickly people catch on to someone who is sneaky. Sheila may think she is clever but if she knew that people were "on" to her and discussing it around the water cooler, she would be humiliated. Sneakiness means the person shouldn't be doing what she's doing or that she doesn't have the strength of character to face someone's displeasure with her idea or plan.

### Dishonesty

Dishonesty is chronic deceitfulness whether it is by commission or omission. It means that a person cannot be trusted, and whether they realize it or not, it also means they cannot trust themselves. Trust and truthfulness are the foundation of integrity; when a person is dishonest, it prevents even his closest friends from feeling comfortable with him. Dishonesty cannot be disguised because it filters into your personality, changes who you are and casts doubt on what you do.

### Failing to acknowledge and apologize for hurtful behavior

This trait is the result of conceit. If a person cannot admit to being wrong, they have a distorted sense of pride. Someone who cannot admit to an occasional blunder or episode of poor judgment is insecure. While people who can't apologize like to convey the impression that they are liked and respected, at an unconscious level, they are fearful people will see them as failures.

People who begin an apology with "If I hurt you . . .," are *not* apologizing. What they are backhandedly saying is, "I'm not going to admit I did anything wrong, but I'll sound remorseful so other people will think I'm a heckuva good person." This violates the people being apologized to because it minimizes their feelings, equality and dignity. Integrity means having to say you're sorry.

### Showing disrespect to people, property and nature

The expression "Who died and made you king?" fits this pattern of behavior because it suits people who believe they are privileged. They operate under the concept of the Divine Right of Kings, behaving however they see fit. They disdain the rest of us as children of a Lesser God, setting themselves above us miserable mortals. Because these people surreptitiously believe that they are above the law, by default others are powerless to stop them. This is a power issue. Desecrating nature is an egregious cosmic transgression that will result in sad and toxic consequences. It is arrogance at its most selfish and obscene. Integrity here means being humble and respecting the environment as well as other human beings.

### Arrogance

This is the sin for which Lucifer was cast out of heaven. It presupposes that a person knows better than anyone else about anything and further, that others are downright tiresome for not being as brilliant. It is lonely up there on Know-It-All Mountain because no one wants a relationship with a person who makes it clear that everyone else is pathetic. The ironic thing about arrogance is that the person usually believes they have an incredible amount of integrity when in realty, they haven't a shred. Integrity is viewing others as equals.

### Closed-mindedness

Someone may be a wonderful person, but if they have no room for other concepts, philosophies and opinions, they deny the diversity that is clearly inherent in all creation. Stubbornly resisting an idea that threatens one's world view rejects the sacred that resides in otherness, in that which is different. There is nothing that says we all must agree, but when a person's goal is to keep their world intact at any price, they are actually saying that their belief is absolute truth. In a sense, it is rejection of otherness in its most base form.

Integrity means understanding the bias we all have for the familiar and knowing we have to be open to hearing the whole story. Integrity does not mean we have to agree with everything; it means we must allow that another person can see things differently.

### Blaming

Blaming demonstrates a lack of maturity and responsibility. Kids blame each other because they don't want to suffer any consequences. When a person blames someone else for something they know they did, they know they have debased the reputation of another. We seem to live in a culture of blaming, all the way from the builder who screws up then blames the workers to a husband who blames his wife for making him hit her. Blaming leaves a symbolic tire mark down the other person's back and a black mark on the accuser's soul. In a book titled *Mistakes Were Made (but not by me)*[40] the authors give many examples of shameless public officials tirelessly blaming others for their own mistakes. Although it may seem obvious, integrity means no excuses, no finger pointing. There is a great deal of respect for people who take responsibility for what they've done and, often, the respect so minimizes the deed that a person actually comes out ahead in the eyes of others.

### Breaking promises

Those most affected by broken promises are children: a divorced parent who regularly misses visitation, a birthday celebration that never materialized, a school play never attended. Our culture yearns for the old fashioned pledge, "You have my word," because it is so seldom heard. The insidious nature of a broken promise is in its very brokenness—for the person whose trust has been shattered, and for the person marred by his own selfishness.

Broken promises mean that the individual has unilaterally decided what she wants to do is more important than what the other person wants or needs. Integrity calls for steadfastness in making promises and keeping the promises made.

## Name-calling

Name-calling is an attempt to destroy another person's identity and grows out of the name caller's inability to make an intelligent point. It is an effort to depersonalize and generalize others by lumping them together under a negative label. There is an ugliness to name-calling; it is treacherous and can to ruin someone. A person of integrity who makes their point with dignity and grace will be imminently more believable than a person who hurls names in a fiery attempt to vilify.

In the end, there are many times, thousands of times, when we act contrary to our higher self. Every one of the behaviors discussed in this chapter separates us from our authentic selves. We are human and by inference, flawed. But our ability to move past our flawedness is based on our desire to honor the holy in ourselves and in others. Thomas Merton, a prominent twentieth century monk, wrote a prayer that is beloved by many because it describes the integrity and earnestness with which we seek God and the confusion that is part of our imperfect humanity:

> My Lord God,
> I have no idea where I am going,
> I do not see the road ahead of me,
> I cannot know for certain where it will end.
> But I believe that the desire to please you
> Does in fact please you.

And I hope that I have that desire
In all that I am doing.
I hope that I will never do anything
Apart from that desire
And I know that if I do this
You will lead me by the right road
Though I may know nothing of it.
Therefore will I trust you always
Though I may seem to be lost
And in the shadow of death.
I will not fear, for you are ever with me
And will never leave me to face my perils alone.

# 13

# Phantom Thinking: Slaying the Ghost

*. . . and she [Alice] had never forgotten that, if you drink too much from a bottle marked 'poison' it is almost certain to disagree with you, sooner or later.*—Alice in Wonderland, Lewis Carroll

As you read this book, it is likely there were ideas that resonated with you more than others. You may have a sense of being carried along by a current of newfound mindfulness or maybe you're drawn to living your life differently, but now what?

The following questions will help you discover the phantom thinking patterns that keep you from creating a way of living that is successful yet reverent of your spirit. These patterns live invisibly in your unconscious and affect you without your even realizing it. All you know is that you "just feel" a certain way but don't really know why. If you bring these phantom thoughts into your consciousness, you can reevaluate the "things" that bother you with a new clarity and recreate your thinking.

Read the following statements, then circle the answer that best describes your thinking *most often*. Everyone thinks at least one of these things at some time or another, so an occasional thought should not be counted. For example, if you answered mostly d's, then go to the section that discusses the "d" responses. If there are two letters that "tie," read both corresponding sections.

The following ideas that correspond to the letters you've chosen will help you understand how these phantom thoughts influence your thinking. They will also show you how to reframe your "self" concept which has been distorted by the Self-Esteem Myth. When you are finished, turn to page 161 for a final thought.

1. a. I watch other people's reaction to me and become nervous if I don't think they like me or approve of what I've said.
   b. No matter what I am doing or where I am, I feel as though I don't belong
   c. I am the strong one in my birth-family
   d. I don't see how anyone could really love me
   e. I like to do two things at once

2. a. There is nothing I'm really good at
   b. I have dreams about living in other places
   c. If I think my family doesn't like something I am doing, it drives me nuts
   d. I don't disagree with my partner even though I think he/she is wrong
   e. Even though I get enough sleep, I still feel tired

3. a. I don't like to take risks
   b. I visited a place I'd never been before yet it felt familiar, like I had once lived there
   c. I feel good about myself until I visit home
   d. My partner is a better person that I am
   e. There isn't enough time to do all the things I'd like

4. a. When someone seems confident it makes me feel worse
   b. I have a sense I should be doing something other than what I am now doing
   c. My parents are/were disappointed in me
   d. If my partner is nice to me, even though I like it, I feel funny
   e. My nerves are raw

5. a. When I'm alone, I use old or plastic dishes because I don't want to dirty the good ones
   b. Even though I have a good job, I hate going in to work every day
   c. When I visit home, I don't tell anyone what I'm really thinking
   d. I always do what my friends want, even if I don't really want to
   e. I spend almost as much time volunteering as I do working

6. a. I tend to feel bad about myself when I read about someone achieving their goal
   b. I made a mistake choosing my career or college major
   c. I will buy something for everyone else in my family rather than for myself
   d. I never go very long without a girlfriend/boyfriend
   e. It bothers me when others don't work as hard as I do

7. a. I don't like competition, even if it's friendly
   b. Sometimes it seems like I spend more time thinking about the work I'd rather be doing than I spend doing my actual job
   c. My parents and siblings are critical of other people
   d. Since I don't have any hobbies, I just go along with whatever my partner wants to do
   e. When I go to bed at night I can't stop thinking about every thing I have to do

8. a. I worry too much about my performance
   b. No matter what job I have, I don't seem happy
   c. It is exhausting to visit home during the holidays
   d. I know I shouldn't, but I keep dating people who aren't good for me
   e. I feel guilty if I'm not doing something

9. a. I feel like I have good ideas but I won't speak up about them
   b. I feel underemployed but can't seem to do anything about it
   c. I feel like I have to plan around what my siblings or parents want
   d. My friends seem to take advantage of me
   e. I can't say "no"

10. a. I would rather play things safe
   b. At work, time just crawls
   c. I am definitely not the black sheep of the family
   d. I spend a lot more money on my friends than they spend on me
   e. I usually run late

**If you chose mostly a's, your phantom thinking is that you are not as good or successful as other people. It keeps you from expressing the passion and creativity that are spilling over, begging to be acknowledged and utilized.**

Your answers indicate you are hesitant to put yourself out there, whether it is voicing your opinion or trying out a new idea. The Myth has infused you with the belief that you are simply not good enough and to try and fail is so shameful and embarrassing that it is best to never take a risk.

Your root belief is that as an individual, you want to be successful, but instead of a sense of adventure or of feeling alive because you have dared to accept the challenge of living deeply, you are filled with the fear of an existential death. On the following pages I have listed ten behaviors that will move you toward a life of living powerfully.

### 1. Take the first step

What you need to do is take that first step—no matter how small. If you are unhappy in your job, then update your resume and if you don't have one, create one. Look in the paper or on the Internet to see which jobs appeal to you. You don't have to get a new job right away . . . just attune your thinking to the idea that there is something better for you. If you keep this thought in the forefront of your mind, you will be less and less intimidated by initiating change.

At some point everyone feels discouraged or foolish when they start down a new path, but growth lies in stretching beyond your comfort zone. The "not trying" is what ultimately produces feelings of impotence because intuitively you know you have lost something valuable by turning your back on opportunity.

## 2. Do not allow yourself to dwell on negative thoughts

The habit of thinking negatively is something you learned at a critical time in your development or in your childhood, or as a result of a bad or traumatizing experience. Instead of processing and coming to terms with the experience, you continued to think the same thing over and over and soon you could not think about it any other way because your brain had been so deeply imprinted. These thoughts then become your truth. You may think "This doesn't happen to other people "or, "I am so 1) incompetent and/or 2) stupid that I should never risk this kind of thing again." It may sound ridiculous when your negative thought is exposed, but phantom fears feel real when you are in the middle of them.

When you have negative thoughts, tell yourself you have a choice: "I can think negatively about this or I can think positively about this. Positive will move me toward the life I want, negative won't." It may seem unlikely, but say it enough times and you will see how engulfed you are in negativity—the first cousin to fear of failing. If you are not able to conquer these negative thoughts, talk to a good friend or see a counselor. People are often reluctant to seek counseling for fear they are going to have to confront a long-held fear, tell a spouse they are unhappy or face unpleasant feelings. Counseling may eventually open you up to those tasks but only when you are ready.

If this describes the feelings you have, don't admonish yourself. Be grateful that you have identified the thinking that has held you back and that you have a plan for changing these mistaken beliefs.

## 3. Determine you will no longer accept your status quo

The important thing is to *do something different*. Make a list of goals you would love to achieve. A life that is pitted with regret is a life that did not explore the opportunities presented to it. Challenges that come to you are challenges which you have either consciously or unconsciously drawn to yourself so you can meet them and move forward.

### 4. Acknowledge each accomplishment

Acknowledge each new accomplishment, no matter how small. For instance, if you are shy but you make a suggestion to your boss, recognize this for what it is—a step toward getting rid of the ghost of failure. In fact, I strongly recommend that you keep a journal, or at least a list of new behaviors, that you can revisit when you think you have made no progress. With each challenge met, no matter how small, you need to remind yourself that you have just moved one step closer your goal. Remember: Success is the foundation of success.

### 5. Visualize

Shakti Gawain, author of many books on creative visualization, stresses the importance of seeing yourself achieving your objectives. Seeing yourself in the role or in the place you think you should be opens your spirit, your physical body and your quantum magnetic field to positive possibilities. You will attract the opportunities to which you aspire. It is not just wishful thinking but rather successful thinking when it is joined with the four other powerful steps outlined here.

Remember, you responded to particular statements in this questionnaire because they resonated with something in you. Listen because your spirit knows what it needs before your conscious self knows.

### 6. Be intentional about allotting time to do what you know you are called to do

Your growing awareness should not be treated like a pesky mosquito buzzing around your head but like an urgent telegram. Daydreaming and putting off until "someday" those things within you that need expression dooms you to a dull and uninteresting life. While you may be doing worthwhile things——raising your children or volunteering at the local shelter—do not be lulled into thinking that's all there is.

After you identify what it is you need to do, figure out a way to incorporate it into the time you have. "I don't have time" is an understandable lament, especially if you are a single parent or a commuter but it is not an ironclad defense. There are weekends, holidays, babysitters or friends who can give you some time off.

You must also set your priorities. If you do the dishes, mow the lawn, clean the garage or shop till you drop there will never be time for your soul. Right now my bed's not made, there's laundry in the dryer and my kitchen counter looks like I just held a garage sale on it because I've been writing all day. All of that "stuff" will get done but the point is that what is truly important gets done first.

You are going to have to turn off the television. It may only be white noise in the background to keep you company but it is noise that drains your spirit. It keeps you from fully submerging yourself in your work and keeps you from being present with yourself.

### 7. Resist the urge to judge your effort or compare yourself to someone else

As was mentioned in chapter six, the chapter on creativity, the bird doesn't sing because someone is listening; it sings because the song is in its heart. The comment I hear so often from people when we are talking about this is that they feel self-indulgent when they pursue something that interests them but doesn't seem to have a goal or use. Even if they do embark on something creative, they wonder what they will do with it, saying things like, "Nobody'll ever buy my paintings," or "everything in my garden dies," or "even if I cook it, no one in this house will eat it." True, you may never sell a painting or have your garden featured in a magazine or get any-body in your family to eat anything other than macaroni and cheese . . . so what? Don't let the Self-Esteem Myth spoil it for you. Start! You will soon understand why you need to do it. In fact, knowing you never have to show your art or have anyone look at your project is liberating. Your creativity will be unfettered because you're not worrying about the outcome.

## 8. Embrace the risk

It *is* risky to move or start a new career or leave a bad marriage. Maybe you are taking a risk by sinking money into a project or dream that has no guarantees. You may not have as much money or security as you have now, but even if it doesn't work out the way you want it to, at least you will know you didn't let the chance to live fully pass you by. Being fully alive means experiencing everything, painful and joyous. Embracing the risk means you will view your desire as a clarion call to live deeply. You will take challenges one at a time and will use the same intelligence and creativity that you utilize for everything else. Life isn't guaranteed but you certainly have a modicum of control in how you plan for things. Don't live with regret, mourn over lost opportunities. This is it. Right now . . . this is your life. Tomorrow isn't your life—today is. Pay attention to your daydreams. Listen to your heart. The truth of who you are meant to be cannot and will not lead you astray. The answer is ceaselessly and unmistakably within.

## 9. Tell someone what you are going to do

Commit yourself publicly so you can't talk yourself out of doing it. Obviously, if it is a bad idea, *everyone* will let you know. Even then, what seems like a bad idea is simply an idea that would scare them if they were going to do it. But they aren't going to do it, you are. Good friends will encourage you. Rid yourself of anyone who is jealous of what you are doing ("You can't do that . . . it'll never work") and wants to stop you. This change and risk business is hard enough as it is; you need to be surrounded by people who love and support you.

## 10. Start today

Go out and buy some supplies; mark your calendar. Take care of the logistics; this might mean clearing out a place for you to work, signing up for a class or talking to a travel agent. But do something TODAY. Even if it's late, you can make a list of what you need to do to get started tomorrow. Give yourself a task for the next day. Most unrealized dreams have drowned in inertia. If you start to falter ask yourself how you would feel if you were to drop the whole idea. If you think you're too old, then think of how old you will be in a year when you haven't pursued your dream. Then think of the one thing that keeps you from starting. You would be amazed at how often the thing we think is going to stand in our way is the most easily solved. Four years of school is not going to shrink into one year but talking to an advisor might open a door you had not considered. Plan one thing each day until you have a good head of steam. It will become exciting and you wouldn't dream of stopping.

**If you answered mostly b's, your phantom thinking has convinced you that you should stay where you are, keeping you in an occupation or an area that conflicts with the nature of who you are and who you are destined to be. In actuality, you are seeking your place in Creation and your spirit will be restless until you find it.**

This is a most exciting condition in which to find yourself. It is as though you have just been given a map to a buried treasure. Parts of the map are faint, the territory is somewhat unfamiliar and there are several trails to the treasure. Sometimes you will think you've made a wrong turn or been mislead by a detour; however, on the Journey, all diversions and mistakes are necessary. The only true mistake is giving up before you reach your destination. Henry David Thoreau's famous quote, "The mass of men lead lives of quiet desperation" may apply to you. It describes a soul that is only going through the motions. You may not feel your life is *awful*, but there is that part of you that feels arid, empty. Having a "sense" that you should be doing something else is a huge, flashing message. It's not a little nagging reminder like "I really need to clean out the garage someday." It is more urgent than that. It is more like, "Wake up! This is your only life. Quite wasting time." Your "sense" is the essence of you; it is your compass and your guide.

Few of us start out in the job of our dreams. We've all heard stories about this famous person who started out selling newspapers or that famous person who was short-order cook. People who are established in their careers, famous and not, frequently speak of the lessons they learned in their first jobs. Work cannot be overlooked as a formative experience for our soul and if it's wrong for us, our soul lets us hear about it in the form of anxiety, restlessness, anger or depression. When you give up, it is most likely when you are not in an optimal place in your life. In other words, giving up too soon is like being stuck in a rut that is only two inches deep but acting as though you are neck-deep in quicksand. The only way you will know whether you are stuck or whether you are in a place of rest and renewal is to pay attention to what your gut tells you. Listen to where your spirit is telling you to go.

These experiences are foundational to you as you begin your quest for the sacred you. Joseph Campbell said, "Follow your bliss and doors will open where there were no doors before." Here are ten ways to start following your bliss.

## 1. Pay attention to when you become stuck

When you find yourself stuck it can be a sign that you are getting close to claiming the work and life God intends for you. Sometimes your spirit is fearful of claiming its rightful place but you can move beyond that fear. Stuckness drains your energy and leaves you feeling heavy; it feels monotonous and hopeless. Yet, stuckness has a message. Sometimes it is a neon clock reminding you that time is ticking by and sometimes it is a red light, warning you to stop and think about what you really want. Maybe you don't want to succeed because it brings more responsibility and accountability. Maybe you are forced to change because a child leaves home or you lose your job.

But, if you embrace the stuckness as a sign pointing the way, you will experience a wisdom moment. While painful, your soul identifies with the deep truths revealed in wisdom moments. Wisdom paints the future on your spirit.

## 2. Don't let the fear of making a decision immobilize you

Fear of moving forward is understandable but unnecessary. One of the things we do to ourselves is calamitize our decisions, believing that once we make a decision, it can never be changed. There is only one thing you can never come back from and that is physical death. Everything is subject to change but Eastern philosophy can teach us much about the cycle of life and death. Unlike us, in Eastern thought the cycle is life, death, life. The death of one part of us gives birth to another.

## 3. Imagine yourself in the place you feel you should be

Visualize yourself being promoted to manager, going back to college, moving to the desert or showing your artwork in a gallery. This is how you "claim" your place, both psychically and emotionally. By "seeing" yourself in the life you desire, you begin to move toward it. You will become more comfortable thinking of your life as different from what it is now. You will find yourself open to changes which you never recognized as opportunities before. Don't become impatient with the process. Everything happens in the time that it should happen.

## 4. Listen to your center

If you know you are in the wrong job, think about the things you have liked doing in the past and begin doing them again. Or, start with something you've always wanted to do, no matter how farfetched. Sometimes when you're doing just what you always do, opportunities drop in your lap. If you're not paying attention, you could miss the opportunity of a lifetime.

A few years ago DuPont aired a compelling commercial about a mistake. A scientist left some chemicals in a beaker overnight. When she came back the next morning they had solidified into a clear substance which took the form of the beaker and remained intact when the beaker was broken. Rather than continuing with her original research, the scientist pursued the development of this new substance which we now know as Lucite.

### 5. Heed the restlessness

From the time I was very young, five or six, I remember looking at my dad's books. I loved to be in the room with the tall bookcases. I used to play with the books, pretend to "read" them, smell the leather bindings and feel the texture of the pages. I would also practice "writing" on discarded yellow-lined paper. I never forgot that experience and somehow knew, even at that early age, that my life and books would forever be intertwined. Even though I successfully pursued several different careers, every time I read, or even held a book, I felt restless. And I knew what the restlessness meant. It stopped when I began writing.

Once you are aware that this restlessness is your soul seeking its place in the Universe, you are on your way. Make a list of all the things you have ever liked to do and think on it. Our destiny is imprinted on our soul and from the time we become aware of our surroundings, we begin to feel a pull toward the life that already dwells in us.

When your spirit leads, follow. You will always be traveling toward your rightful place; you will always be on your way home.

### 6. Who are you? Which path are you meant to follow?

Obviously if it were as easy as asking and answering this question, you wouldn't be reading this. There would be no anticipation, no surprises, no exhilaration. This would be a tragedy because it is precisely the mystery and the exploration and the wrong turns that make life magical. Kids fantasize about what they are going to be when they grow up and grown ups muse about what comes next. How dull it would be if you knew from the beginning exactly what you were going to be. There would be no daydreaming, no aspirations, only the slow, anticlimactic march toward what you are going to do the rest of your life.

Finding out who you are and what you are to do for your life's work becomes clearer with each life and work experience even though it may not be immediately apparent to you. The question you need to ask yourself is, "What do I feel drawn to? This is the secret. What you are drawn to is what your passion is. You don't have to do something you don't like. It's okay to do what you love!

Pursue your passion and you will know the answer to these questions of who you are and what path you should follow. Pursue your passion and everything else will eventually follow. Maybe not in the beginning, but ultimately, it will, no matter how impossible it seems.

## 7. Be realistic about your capabilities

Our culture doesn't seem to value working one's way up the ladder any more. Print ads and television show very young people in top management positions or living in expensive homes, giving the impression that a great career and big money is easy to come by. Well, it isn't and if you think that when you start out you should be the boss, you aren't being sensible, rational or logical.

Find out what it takes to hold a higher position and work toward that. Sometimes, it's about the number of years you work or how much experience you have and sometimes it's about education or specialized skills. Complaining and blaming only shifts you further from your goal. Learn from the old-timers, if there is such a thing anymore. Respect those under you—they're probably running the organization anyway.

If you want to sing but you aren't very good, take lessons. If the dog howls when you sing, reevaluate. You may end up connected to music in some form but it's probably not going to be singing. Remember, if you're not *meant* to have a certain kind of life, no matter how glamorous, you will be miserable in the long run. It wouldn't be long before you would be right back where you started, feeling restless and unhappy.

## 8. Be aware of the Sacred in your calling

If you are miserable in your job because you think the work is beneath you, there is a truth to learn about the value of work. That truth is that all honest work has value and dignity. If you perform your job with integrity, no one will think less of you for what you do; in fact, they will only respect you for giving your best.

The being miserable referred to here is the type of unhappiness that you feel when you know you are not working up to your capability. If you want to work with computers, but take a job as a security guard because you're afraid you'll fail, this is working beneath your potential. However, if you are a nighttime security guard because you discovered you hate working with computers and want the time to study geology, then you are not working beneath your potential but toward it.

The difficulty with work comes when you stay in a position too long. It stifles your potential. Having a good job but hating to go in everyday is your soul putting you on notice that it's time to move on. If you spend your days thinking about doing something else, pay attention. Restlessness and discontent are actually motivators and without them you might never leave your comfort zone.

If you are held back by the fear of losing insurance coverage or seniority in a retirement plan, continue to make plans but bide your time and do the research. There are many people who make disastrous decisions because they are impatient.

Meanwhile, waiting doesn't mean that your life has to be on hold. It means you turn to hobbies or volunteering or community work as an outlet for your gifts.

The solemn issue is that your ability to impact humankind is contained in your potential. Your longing to create, to serve, to achieve is contained within your potential. So is your passion and a sense of profound contentment. Your potential, your fundamental energy, is the reason for your existence and the seed that will create the rest of your life.

## 9. Don't be afraid of the "C" word

All of the situations mentioned in the "b" questions have one obstacle in common: Change. Change is a core fear for human beings. It is hard. It is scary. It is uncertain. But it can be your friend. Change restores, renews and invigorates. It allows you to experience new energy sparked by overcoming challenges. You must not fear Change, but embrace it as it is the key to all growth.

Some people go to great lengths to keep change from occurring not only because they feel their authority is threatened but because to some, it feels like life and death. They become defensive, block out suggestions, berate those who want to try something new. They manipulate people and circumstances so things stay the same. What they find is that change happens anyhow. Neighborhoods change, new methods come along and old ones become extinct. Kids move away, the workplace becomes automated and spouses leave anyway.

There was a study conducted about fifteen years ago to identify factors common to people who lived to be 100 years or older. One by one the factors the researchers thought might contribute to long life were eliminated. It didn't seem to matter if these folks had a shot of whiskey a day or never drank; if they ate meat every day or vegetables. Slept five hours a night or twelve. In the end, there was only one variable that all the centenarians had in common: Adaptability. When things changed, they rolled with it. They embraced the "new ways" and didn't belittle innovative ideas. Even if their bodies couldn't be as active as they would have liked, their minds were open.

The aspect of acceptance that was most touching was that of being the last one standing. Some of the people they interviewed had lost every member of their family and all of their old friends, yet they continued to make new ones. These centenarians were often the most loved in the nursing home. In fact, the journalist presenting this segment was set to interview a woman when he found out her closest friend had died the night before. He expected that she would want to cancel the interview but she insisted, saying that life must go on.

And it is so . . . life will go on, with or without you. Better to be open to the new and have some say in your life than come late to the party and miss out on cake. To be a reluctant traveler is to turn your back on the gratification and wonder that comes with growth. Will it be painful at times? Of course. Will it be worth it? What do you think?

## 10. Ignore what others think

On the surface, this may sound like very a bad suggestion, but there is a difference between thoughtful or seasoned advice and what someone *thinks.* Unless you have a strong history of making bad decisions, at times it is best to ignore what people want you to do. A funny thing happens when you take risks . . . other people get jealous because they don't want to be reminded of the chances they have passed up. "Invest in beach property in Mexico? Ha, I've got some property in the Everglades I'd like to sell you." But if you've done your research it might well be the move that will change your life; meanwhile, they're still in the same old rut they were in when you first told them about your idea.

Your relatives and friends probably won't find your decision to leave medicine to run a hot dog stand a good one. But maybe your hot dog stand will turn into lots of hot dog stand which create opportunities for others who have no work. Only you can say "Yes," to your potentiality. In the end, it is not others who will live your life, it is you.

**If you have chosen mostly c's, you don't think you can be yourself because your family would disapprove. These leftover tapes keep you from believing you deserve support, love, success and happiness.**

Family loyalty issues are intense, unavoidable and usually invisible. I am not referring to your teen years when it is your developmental task to defy everything conventional. I am referring to later in your life when you are in your twenties and thirties, when you have worked through your rebelliousness. It is when you have begun your adult life that you become painfully conscious that you want to make decisions that go against "the way the family does it."

When you spend Christmas with your spouse's family instead of yours, when you take a job and move away, or marry someone your mom or dad disapproves of, or choose a career that they are uncomfortable with, or discipline your children differently, or go to a different church, or don't go to church . . .chances are you're going to hear about it. The bottom line is, to live fully you must give yourself permission to differ with your nuclear family.

Sometimes it's not that much of a problem but sometimes it is wrenching, like being the reason the family business is put up for sale because you have chosen not to take it over.

Each time you make a decision that mollifies someone else's potential disappointment in you, you deny your essential *Self*. There are times when noble decisions are made for the right reasons but this is about giving up your dreams because someone in the family disapproves.

By answering yes to these questions, your need to please others first has grown into a daily drama that represents your desire to be nurtured. By taking care of others you are hoping someone will take care of you—like you wanted to be taken care of by your family. Your innate belief is that you don't have permission to deserve the things you need. You are disappointed that your family doesn't care for you the way you care for them but you accept it because, oh yeah, you don't deserve it anyway. If this is where you find yourself, here are steps you can take to break away from the grip of destructive family loyalty issues.

### 1. Identify the loyalty issues in your family and acknowledge how they affect you

Familial patterns unconsciously motivate us to look for people who are similar to our family. It is commonplace for someone who comes from a family with a history of alcoholism, to end up in a relationship with an alcoholic. You may find yourself attracted again and again to someone who treats you badly because that is the way you were treated. While these may not seem to be loyalty issues at first glance, they illustrate that you have absorbed the message of who your family needs you to be: "Sally never could make good choices," "Dick couldn't stand up for himself." To choose a good spouse or leave a job that is toxic for you, you may have to first break free of the role you were given and have played out thus far in your life. If your role was a healthy one, this won't be an issue for you, but something else might.

Often people will say they were treated wonderfully by their parents but they still engage in destructive relationships. Upon closer examination they might discover that it wasn't how they were treated, it was what they absorbed. In a family of Mideastern descent, girls may be revered but not valued. Or, in a rough and tumble family it may be quite clear that boys don't become nurses and girls shouldn't waste money going to college.

The movie *Saturday Night Fever* is an excellent example of family expectations. Father Ralph is a priest because that is what his parents wanted him to be. His mother, especially, lived through him. Father Ralph began to have doubts about his call to the priesthood. Each time he came home, the charade drained the life from him, his energy sapped by the pretense of being a fulfilled priest; the burden of being someone he was not was slowly killing him. When he finally told his family he was leaving the priesthood, he might as well have announced that he was an ax murderer.

Father Ralph may be an exaggerated example of family loyalty but when your parents have helped you set up a business or put you through college, it is almost unthinkable to them that you might change your mind. You are placed in your roles not only by your family, but by your extended families—friends, spouses, fans. Once you can see how you are affected and by which attitudes and expectations, you are ready to move to the next step.

## 2. Recognize that guilt is normal but transient

Again, *Saturday Night Fever* does a good job portraying the guilt associated with going against family wishes. Father Ralph had known for a long time that he couldn't be a priest any longer. When Ralph told his younger brother, Tony, who didn't much care about anything as long as it didn't mess up his hair, that he was going to leave, even Tony got upset and tried to talk him out of it. His mother pleaded with him, his dad blew up and when he finally left the house, they were in shock. He told his now silent mother and father that he didn't know when he'd be back; the guilt of facing them again was simply too intense.

When you make a disappointing decision, what really happens is that your family's *own* fear of loss makes them want to talk you out of your choice, using a most effective tool . . . guilt. Families panic at the thought you will no longer be the person they've always known, that you are making a mistake or that they will lose their status. Sometimes they feel betrayed and their anguish smothers you like a shroud.

The family will eventually adjust and you will eventually feel at peace with yourself—even if it doesn't work out like you thought. There is no crueler torture than regretting something you didn't do. Years after the opportunity has passed, your soul will continue to wail at the lost possibilities. While you may think the easiest way to avoid the whole mess is to give in and give up, you would be wrong. The feeling you would become intimately acquainted with from that point on would be resentment.

This is particularly true when you watch family members go about *their* life as they want to, hardly remembering what it was you had wanted to do. Meanwhile, you will not be going about your life as you had wanted *and* you will be haunted by "what ifs." As harsh as it sounds, you cannot allow this guilt to stop you; in fact, you may need counseling to see you through this phase of the process.

### 3. Acknowledge this call to your deeper self as part of a larger plan

Few of us are born knowing what our calling is but each of us plays an irreplaceable role in the life of the universe. Being in the wrong place metaphysically deprives us not only of our destiny but deprives the world as well. Had Christopher Columbus bowed to the pressure that he would sail off the edge of the earth, most of us would be sitting in Europe now. And would our country be united if Abraham Lincoln decided after his first defeat he'd never run for office? What if Emily Dickinson had not written 1,700 poems because she decided that since she was confined to her house for most of her life, she had nothing to write about?

While in retrospect these individuals made decisions that impacted millions of people, at the time they had to wrestle with their own doubts. They all had reasons not to choose their destiny—ridicule, failure, disappointment—yet they chose it anyway.

By now you are probably wondering what your destiny is and thinking, "I don't have a clue."

You find out what you are supposed to do by doing—not by living your life robotically. Your calling may not be anything definitive in your eyes, but it is *your* calling and that makes it important. It may take years to understand the events in your life and what you have been called to, but that does not excuse you from making yourself available to become who and what you are meant to be. And don't think that because you've embarked on this marvelous adventure that you'll never be discouraged. This is a journey—not a holiday in Fiji. Journeys are fraught with anxiety and doubts, but they are also profoundly joyful and inspiring.

### 4. Differentiate!

As noted in an earlier chapter, one of the hardest things we have to do as adults is to make a distinction between ourselves and our family. Not only must we make the distinction but sooner or later we must act on it. That is what it means to differentiate. We have to see where the family ends and we begin. Each person is an individual who experiences the world differently than anyone else. For a parent or sibling to expect that you will see things exactly as they do is emotionally immature. Same goes for you. For you to punish them for not agreeing with your expectations is selfish.

This is not about your parent's expectation that you should be honest or have integrity. Those expectations are foundational. It is about living the life you are called to live. As mentioned earlier in this book, love is the desire to see a person's world grow, not shrink. Once you understand the dynamics of this differentiation process, you are ready to begin the journey. Does this mean you dump your family or disown your roots? No, it means that you must acknowledge how you are different and claim it.

Feeling guilty about a career choice or being drained of energy when you go home are all signs that you have not given yourself permission to *be* yourself. Screw up your courage and state what it is you want and then remain firm. It probably will not be pleasant, but it will certainly be worth it.

### 5. Honor the sacredness of your life

If you have trouble validating yourself for your own sake, think of the people you will affect in your lifetime. You *will* make a difference to someone; you will vitalize a spirit, engender hope, comfort loss, create beauty, save a life, create a life. Whether you want to acknowledge it or not, you are ultimately pledged to a greater good and it is your sacred responsibility to respond to it through the desire that lives in your heart. The path may seem crooked, but you will eventually understand where you are going.

### 6. There is no Fairy Godmother

What you have to accept is that no one else is going to wave a magic wand to make this conflict with your family go away. You will not feel the confidence and self-love that you long for if you continue to believe you are powerless. You have learned that you are not sufficient; the key to reversing your thinking is to accept that you *do* have the power to be different. You may need counseling to get through it, but you eventually can do this. However, acceptance is just part of the equation. The other part is your determination to change. You don't have to have all the answers when you begin but you do need to resolve that you will stick with it; this transition *will* happen in time.

### 7. Put the oxygen mask on yourself first

If you are hurting as much as some of your answers indicate, the fact is right now you are a bottomless vessel that will never be full until you accept that your family dynamics do not have to dictate the rest of your life. Playing out the family code will only continue to deprive your Self and will further deplete your starving soul. A gaunt inner essence cannot nourish and give birth to the miracles within you.

Flight attendants tell you that if you travel with a dependent, it is critical that you put the oxygen mask on yourself first. If you don't, you won't live long enough to tend to the other person. You gradually become oxygen deprived if you don't free yourself from family expectations; you must put the oxygen mask on yourself first.

Feeling deprived because of what you learned growing up is like sitting before a feast but not eating. The very fact that you are living on this earth entitles you to pick up that knife and fork. When you feel like backing down, remember that in most cases your family just needs time to adjust to new ideas about you. Others have lived perfectly fine lives after standing up to their families; you can, too.

### 8. Eliminate the people who don't value you

When you don't value yourself, others pick up on it and won't value you either. It is difficult to reverse a lifelong, negative self-belief if you associate with people who reinforce it. It is especially difficult when these people are relatives. If you are in close proximity to someone who devalues you, the first thing you must do is to shift away or detach yourself from them while you mend. In fact, this is an excellent first exercise in changing your opinion of yourself.

Think about it—what obligation do you have to listen to someone who is rude, mean or abusive to you? If you have tolerated this behavior because you are afraid you will end up alone, consider that your own company has got to be better than the company of people who quite obviously don't care about you. Make sure if Aunt Ruth is at a family gathering that you stay engaged with others, giving her only a nod or hello. If your relatives persist in trying to control you, *you persist.*

Of course, if it is a spouse who is abusive, sometimes just letting him know you will not tolerate the abuse any longer will get his attention. Tell him that you will leave the room or hang up if he starts in, and then do it. You don't have to be nasty, just firm. If there are any threats, spoken or unspoken, of physical retaliation, run, don't walk to your nearest relative, domestic abuse center, pastor, friend or therapist since the abuse intensifies when an abuser feels threatened or abandoned.

This is a particularly dangerous time and you will need other trained people to help you through it. Trust your gut on this. If you feel threatened, you must get help. Don't tell yourself it's all in your head. If your gut is warning you, to heck with your head.

## 9. Surround yourself with positive and supportive people

Yes, they are out there. Once you find them, there are two things you need to do. First, spend more time with people who are respectful and supportive of you. Second, spend more time with people who are respectful and supportive of you.

Sometimes you have to make new friends to fill the void left by branching out from your family. It is critical because it will keep you from reverting to destructive patterns. This can be intimidating but if you're shy, smile at someone who also seems shy, or join in a conversation or become active in a cause that you feel passionate about or take somebody to lunch or join a gym.

These suggestions sound simplistic but they are down to earth and do work. You don't have to do everything at once. Just start making new friends one opportunity at a time. You may just be an answer to prayer for someone else.

### 10. Take control

Taking control is difficult if your family sent you the message that you are invisible because then you don't exist and, therefore, could not have physical or emotional needs. This pattern is discernible when you're in a car that is uncomfortably hot to you, but you won't ask to open the window. It happens when your medium-rare steak comes out well done and you don't send it back.

You do not need anyone's permission to advocate for yourself. Just because this is the way you have been up until now, it does not mean you have to continue. When you do assert yourself, be prepared for a backlash. Breaking old patterns means people have to adjust to the fact that they cannot treat you the way they have always treated you. Your changes will inconvenience them which they won't like.

You have accepted the victim role (I can't) long enough and now you're on your way to reject it. How? Get a new friend who loves you to role- play with you. Take an assertiveness class. Read a book on assertiveness, my favorites being an old classic, *When I Say No, I Feel Guilty*, by Manuel J. Smith and *Your Perfect Right*, by Alberti and Emmons. This process of revaluing yourself (or perhaps valuing yourself for the first time) will seem strange at first but, then, everything new does. Remind yourself that this is the only life you have—there are no do-overs. You can choose to be controlled by someone else or you can choose to be happy.

**If you answered mostly d's, you have become an empty shadow of your partner and friends. Edna St. Vincent Millay, a modern poet, gave a poignant description of losing oneself as "a pool, a tepid little pool, drying inward from the edge."**

Somewhere along the line, you lost confidence in yourself. Maybe someone belittled you when you expressed an opinion. Or possibly you were trained to give in when you contradicted someone else's beliefs. Or perhaps you were starved emotionally and morphed into someone you weren't. *Someone* gave you the impression that your ideas were not good or not welcomed. Whatever the reason, you may now find yourself functioning as a "twin" to your partner or doormat to your friends. If you've answered the questions in the first part of the chapter and were interested enough to turn to this section, you must want something different than what you now have. The following measures should help you get started on becoming more yourself and less like someone else.

### 1. Look in the mirror . . . really, stop and go look in the mirror

This person looking back at you deserves to be secure and happy. This person looking back at you has all the essential qualities to be in a good relationship. But before this happens, you have to be honest with yourself. *You need to get your own life.* Maybe you never had your own life or maybe you lost touch with it over the years but you have to look back at your reflection and vow, "This is it . . . starting from this moment I am on a mission."

When children are missing, swarms of people volunteer to find them and bring them back. Do you deserve any less? You were created with a unique personality, a personality meant to impact the lives of others. You must acknowledge that you are important enough to warrant a search for yourself before any of the following steps begin to make sense.

### 2. To blame or not to blame

The point is, you don't have to work through how you got where you are and who is responsible in order to make the necessary changes in your relationships. While the concept of counseling is discussed elsewhere in this book, it is only *mentioned*. The impor-

141

tant piece of this is that you are in control, not someone who said something that once that hurt you. There will always be plenty of blame to go around but it is not helpful. What is helpful is knowing what needs to be fixed and how to go about fixing it. To hang on to old business is an excuse not to change.

### 3. Assess the relationship

The first thing you need to decide: Is your relationship so fragile that it will shatter if you don't participate in your partner's activities? Will you face an argument if you don't agree with your partner on everything? Will your friends fail to include you if you stand up for what you want?

If the answer is yes, my guess is you already know these are destructive relationships and that you are putting off the painful and scary task of confronting them. The second thing to ask yourself is, "Is this relationship worth it?" Is this kind of daily humiliation preferable to being alone? If you do not face this issue now, five years from now you will end up in the same kinds of relationships because, what has changed? Why would you behave the same way as you always have and expect something different?

Now, if your partner or friend would not be upset if you began to reshape things, then staying in a supportive situation will help you focus your efforts on yourself. Yet even in a supportive situation, be prepared for unexpected changes that we will address in step eight.

### 4. Reintroduce yourself to you

Remember what you were like when you were ten . . . fourteen . . . eighteen? You may not be as far from that person as you think. What did you want your life to be? What did you want to do? What were you excited about? We are finding that late childhood and adolescence are markers for who we are on our passage into adulthood. The seed of who we were then does not just dry up and float away.

What were your dreams then? What are your dreams now? Fulfilled dreams depend on you. No one else. *You* are the knight in shining armor.

You must reintroduce the you who used to dream big dreams to the you who has lost sight of them. You must be constantly conscious of your imaginings. If you keep that vision of what you want in the forefront and think optimistically about it, you will recognize opportunities that can bring it about. If you have a dream but figure there is no way it is ever going to happen, opportunities will go over your head that you didn't recognize as opportunities. Even those times in your life that were painful and lonely gave you strength, even if you don't recognize it, that is available to you now.

## 5. Getting a Life

We all know what it means when someone says, "Get a Life!" It means that you have too much time on your hands to be interested in nit-picky stuff. This is *not* what it means here.

What it means is that you've lost sight of your own meaningfulness. You've lost sight of what you want to do in your lifetime. You have become focused on another person to the exclusion of yourself. You are consistently putting another's person's needs before your own to the point where you don't have a life without this person.

So here comes the list. Make a list (yes, really write it down . . . don't skip this step!) of everything you want in your life and everything you want to experience while you are on this earth. I know what some of you will say. You'll say you don't know and can't come up with anything. This may be true at first but I challenge you to dream big. You don't have to figure out how it's going to happen. And please, please, don't say it can never happen.

Grandma Moses took up painting in her seventies! Do you want to finish college? Do you want to open your own business? Do you want to learn to change your oil or cook? Include every single thing . . . and add to your list as you think of things.

This is your treasure map. Keep it where you can see it daily—in your pocket, at your desk, in the bathroom. But look at it every-day. This method has recently seen a lot of publicity but it has actually been around for quite a while and the reason is, it works. This single action will open you to possibilities and solutions that can create the life you want to live.

## 6. Tackle your deepest fear

Until you face what keeps you in an unproductive behavior pattern, you will be haunted by this lingering fear and it will continue to block you from making the changes you need to make. Here are some of the more common fears:

a. My partner won't like me if he/she knew the real me
b. I'll lose the relationship if I change it now
c. I'm afraid to be alone so I'd rather have a bad relationship than none at all
d. I'm not strong enough to do this
e. It's not really that bad
f. He/she is going to get really angry
e. People will say I'm controlling/pushy/wrong/selfish

While your concerns may have some truth to them, the fact is that all of the above examples have one thing in common: They all imply that *you don't count.* Your thoughts don't count, your opinions don't count, your needs don't count, your selfhood doesn't count. If you don't decide to change your behavior, over the course of time one of two things will happen. The feelings you have now will get progressively worse. You will steadily begin to despise the people who don't care about you and you will despise yourself for being dependent on those people.

The other thing that can happen is that you become more and more passive, slipping into a low-grade, lifelong depression.

Changing personal mind-sets and behavior patterns is kind of like not wanting to jump off a pier. Jumping becomes much more attractive if the pier is on fire. Guess what? If you're reading this now, your pier is on fire.

Each time you reach inside, take a little risk and survive, you have come one step closer to reclaiming yourself. If you know a situation is coming up that feels challenging, run it by a close friend, get some ideas about how to handle it. If something came up and you didn't do very well, talk to the friend again and consider the experience a rehearsal for the next time. There is no magic formula; Nike's advice fits quite well here. Just do it. Behavior can change attitudes when attitudes don't change behavior.

## 7. Discuss your feelings with your partner or friend

You may shrink from this suggestion, finding it the most difficult part of this whole experience but this step is critical. If you are reluctant, write out what you want to say and practice it. If you have to have a cheat sheet in your pocket, that's fine. If you sense it is an unsafe thing to do, don't make yourself a target. If this is the case for you, you have a bigger problem and you need to seek help beyond this book.

So, the purpose of doing this is not to blame anyone; you, your partner or your friend, but to acknowledge how the pattern of losing yourself in the relationship began, the damaging effects it has had on you and your partner and what you want to do about it.

One of the problems in changing behaviors within a relationship is that the other persons may feel like the rug has been pulled out from under them. When we first begin a relationship, we have an idea of how each of us should behave. Over time, things may begin to erode and the relationship is not what we want but, nonetheless, we understand there was an agreement, usually unspoken, about how things are supposed to play out. When it changes, as it most invariably does, the most common reaction is to feel betrayed. After all, your partner or friend probably feels like she has kept up her end of the deal and now, because of you, the rules are going to change. She is going to have to forfeit some of the benefits she has come to enjoy.

If you want to give up the job that pays the bills and go back to school, your spouse will have to adjust his style of living. If you decide that you really hate living in Kalamazoo and want to move to Atlanta, your partner would have to pull up roots, too. Hashing it out and coming to a decision is what happens in relationships. It is most successful if it occurs between two equals. You *are* an equal; you must remember this and act upon it because the fulfillment of your life does depend on it.

## 8. The healing powers of change

This is a reminder that change is normal, necessary and healthy. Just because you started out with a particular pattern in your relationship doesn't mean you have forever forfeited the opportunity to change it. In fact, maybe the other person would welcome your new emotional independence. Maybe he or she is relieved you are finally speaking out and is looking forward to not shouldering all the responsibility for the relationship. Marriages can disintegrate when one person bears the burden of being "everything" to their partner. Friendships become distorted when one person always needs something from the other.

Refusal to change when change is needed is toxic. When one partner doesn't have emotional space because the other person is so needy, there will eventually be some type of break in the relationship. Either emotional intimacy will die or anger and/or resentment will grow. Many times I hear this very lament, "I *want* her to tell me what she doesn't like. I *want* somebody who's strong and has her own interests." What your partner wants is intimacy, not shallowness and dependency. What your friend wants is an equal friend, not someone who tolerates cruel behavior and whom she doesn't respect. Change is good, even when it hurts. Change is the one constant in our lives and those who learn to adapt to change live longer and happier lives.

If your partner or friend reacts negatively, if you feel threatened or frightened by your partner's behavior, take it more slowly and make sure you are safe no matter what it takes, even if it means leaving. While you may have been the needy one, sometimes when the tables are turned, it becomes apparent that your partner or friend may have actually been the dependent one. The abusive person often fights to keep the status quo in an sadistic relationship. As discussed earlier, if you get to that point, remember that jealous and insecure people become most dangerous at the point of separation. If this is the case with you, you will need aid and support to keep yourself and family safe.

## 9. Me, myself and I

Two of the questions you may have answered in the quiz were "I never go very long without a girlfriend/boyfriend" and "I know I shouldn't, but I keep dating people who aren't good for me." While this was discussed in chapter eight, it is worth noting again the importance of being able to be alone. Of course, no one wants to be alone, at least, not for long. But one must be *willing* to be alone for any relationship to be viable. If the relationship is wrong for whatever reason, if you are not willing to walk away from it to fix it, or leave if it cannot be fixed, then you are a prisoner.

For some of you, being alone is like standing on the edge of a deep canyon in the dark. You feel panicky and afraid, almost as though you might die. This will not happen. You are basing your perception on how you feel at the moment. Right now, you don't feel so good about yourself and it seems impossible that you could ever be happy without someone.

The question I have for you is did it ever occur to you that you could be *happier* without someone?

Right now you might not even remember what it is like to be fascinated by life. You can't remember how exciting it feels to be absorbed with possibilities that haven't been sacrificed for someone else. You don't know how deeply fulfilling your own company can be. Feelings of fear, worry and anxiety, can be replaced by a peace that is worth far more than anything you think you are losing.

## 10. Don't back down

Talking about changing your habits and doing it are two different things. The difficulty is maintaining a determined attitude in the face of opposition, whether it's because your partner or friend isn't cooperating or you are fearful that you will lose everything. In situations where you are changing the status quo, remember that the equilibrium of the relationship is not only going to be out of balance but can get worse before it gets better. It takes a while to change and some of the time you'll be successful and some of the time you won't. Over time, however, little changes and small victories add up.

Remember, the bottom line is that every time you shrink from being yourself, you are throwing a shovel of dirt onto your spirit. If you participate in the relationship as though you no longer exist, you have as good as proclaimed that you don't matter. You will remain a Stepford spouse, an automaton, living only to please, perennially numb inside. If you don't like this description of yourself, good! Ask yourself candidly, "Do I really want to live like this the rest of my life? Is what I would gain by keeping things the way they are worth losing me?" If it isn't, and I doubt that ever would be, then don't allow yourself to be dead and buried another minute. Life awaits.

**If you answered mostly e's, your phantom thinking will not allow your spirit to rest. You run on adrenaline and when it finally drains from your system, you are exhausted because you have nothing else to sustain you.**

The deeper question here is why is your spirit reluctant to be still? Maybe you believe you aren't worthy or that you have to earn your right to 'be' every single day of your life. Maybe you think that if you know everything and do everything, you are finally enough.

Unconsciously you may believe that busyness is proof that you matter. After all, if you are central to so many organizations and projects, then obviously you are necessary and valuable. This phantom belief puts you in danger of being so busy that you miss your 'real' life.

You are also the kind of person who hates to ask for help. Asking for help implies vulnerability and vulnerability implies that you are not strong and independent. Our culture has convinced us that being independent and asking for help are mutually exclusive. Setting yourself up as the strong one imprisons you in self-imposed isolation from the comfort and support of others. The fear of being exposed as anything but strong is rooted in the need to convince people that you have everything under control and that you don't need them.

## 1. Take an inventory of who and what influences your "busy" actions

You will probably like this exercise because it appeals to your basic need to get busy with something. Grab a piece of paper and make a list with four columns. *It doesn't have to be perfect.* In the first column, write down the influential people in your life; parents, teachers, current or former spouses, colleagues, relatives, friends, children. Also include circumstances that seem to influence your behavior.

Now, in the second column, next to each name or situation, write down how you feel when you are (or were) with that person, or in that situation; for instance, "comfortable" or "inferior" "judged" "accepted."

In the third column, explain why you feel the way you do—for instance, "sister always thought she was better than me" or "Fred criticizes people behind their backs." This takes a little soul searching and may take awhile if you are honest. Decide if the negative

| Who | Feeling | Why | Reaction |
|---|---|---|---|
| Mom | Uncomfortable | Never good enough | I ignore her |
| Dad | Nervous | Compares me to Sis | Anxious, try to please |
| Groups | Embarrassed | I am ugly | I avoid groups |

feelings you experience are legitimate or simply habits. Frequently we don't stop to examine our feelings and we especially don't entertain the prospect that we could ever get rid of or change those feelings. But we *can*. Think about whether the price you pay to continue to feel the same way is worth it.

In the fourth column, identify how this makes you feel, especially if it causes you to feel like you need to do more in order to be accepted.

### 2. Map out how you will act differently around these negative situations and people.

Now add a fifth column. In that column, write down what you can do differently.

| Who | Feeling | Why | Reaction | New behavior |
|-----|---------|-----|----------|--------------|
| Mom | Uncomfortable | Never good enough | I ignore her | Act as if I am good enough |
| Dad | Nervous | Compares me to Sis | Anxious, try to please | Only please if I want |
| Groups | Embarrassed | I am ugly | I avoid groups | People don't really notice me |

Behavior can change attitudes. Even if you don't believe in yourself at first, *behave differently*. There is a scene in *To Kill A Mockingbird* where Scout, an eight-year-old girl, has to walk by the cemetery in the dark. She is petrified but walks by humming and singing to herself as if she weren't scared. Acting *as if* is called whistling past the graveyard, like Scout did. Sometimes willing yourself to have a different attitude doesn't work. But acting *as if* lets you to experience what it is like to be different even if you don't *feel* different.

If you don't start slowing down and paying attention to yourself, you will be perpetually tired and empty. You'll feel as though you have no personal significance without your activities and then you will be afraid *not* to have any activities. You'll be like the executive who retires and then sinks into a black depression because all he had, all he was, was his job.

Determine that you will not volunteer when no one else raises their hand. Decide that you will do only two errands a day—even if it gives your sister an opportunity to complain that *she* would have dropped your sweater off to you if you had left it at *her* house. One situation at a time, one victory at a time is what you are aiming for.

### 3. Be responsible for your activities

Grab another piece of paper. Make a list of all of your obligations. After you have done this, circle the ones that are necessary, important or meaningful to *you*. Now cross off the rest. Think of how you would feel if you didn't have to do the things you crossed off your list. If you feel relief, then you are probably burning your candle at both ends and whatever good this activity is supposed to be doing, it is probably falling miserably short.

Try this experiment: Make out your calendar putting the things you like to do in first.

| 8:00 | Walk | 2:00 | |
|------|------|------|------|
| 9:00 | | 3:00 | |
| 10:00 | | 4:00 | |
| 11:00 | | 5:00 | |
| Noon | Visit favorite bookstore | 6–8:00 | |
| 1:00 | | 8–9:00 | Watch favorite TV shows |
| | | 10:00 | Read to fall asleep |

Next put in the things you absolutely must do.

| | | | |
|---|---|---|---|
| 8:00 | Walk | 2:00 | Office |
| 9:00 | Return calls | 3:00 | Office |
| 10:00 | Grocery store | 4:00 | Office |
| 11:00 | | 5:00 | Office |
| Noon | Visit favorite bookstore | 6–9:00 | Dinner, clean up |
| 1:00 | | 9–10:00 | Watch favorite TV shows |
| | | 10:00 | Read to fall asleep |

Finally, put in things you have volunteered for or feel like you need to do.

| | | | |
|---|---|---|---|
| 8:00 | Walk | 2:00 | Office |
| 9:00 | Return calls | 3:00 | Office |
| 10:00 | Grocery store | 4:00 | Office |
| 11:00 | *Volunteer at school* | 5:00 | Office |
| Noon | Visit favorite bookstore | 6–9:00 | Dinner, clean up |
| 1:00 | *Write thank-you notes* | 9–10:00 | Watch favorite TV shows |
| | | 10:00 | Read to fall asleep |

As you can see, when you schedule time for yourself first and then schedule around it, *you end up getting time for yourself!* This is an effective way of becoming intentional about your activities and breaking the habit of running all the time. As you go along, you will find that you won't be able to fit everything in, which is the point.

When you are emotionally exhausted, you might not be aware that your are lacking balance. Not enough down time or not enough family time or too much volunteer time leaves you feeling sapped and trapped. You know that life is zooming by—yet there is always another chore to do or person to call before you can sit down and rest.

You may not be able to control everything but you can certainly control some things. No one else is going to say, "Poor Sally—don't do this and this and this. You've done enough; now come and sit down." *You* are the one who has to say, "Sally, take a break. It can wait until tomorrow." You are the one responsible for yourself and your schedule. You may need to consider a different job, sharing a commute, moving, or having a frank talk with those who aren't doing their share. You may decide you can't wash the clothes *and* fold them *and* put them away. Maybe it's better to have someone else cut the lawn or clean.

One year I remember being so profoundly exhausted by the time Christmas came that I decided something had to change. I made up my mind that I was not going to send Christmas cards anymore because the task was enormous and even though it was meaningful, I hated doing it. I also decided that we would not go anywhere or have anyone over for dinner on Christmas day—in fact, I would not even cook dinner! Instead, we would have a great dinner the night before and eat leftovers the next day. And (this is my favorite) I would not get out of my pajamas one minute before 5:00 P.M., and sometimes not even then!

The next Christmas was one of our best—the kids loved being able to play without having to clean up or go anywhere and I was able to actually enjoy the day and reflect on its meaning. Twenty years later, we still celebrate Christmas the same way and I still look forward to it. Friends or family who drop by know they will find me in my robe and a self-serve buffet on the table. I restored balance to a part of my life that had gotten out of control.

## 4. *Give* appropriately, *according to your personality type*

Too much giving is not a virtue; it deprives the spirit of the ability to give in the future. If you give and give and end up more energized than before, then you aren't giving too much. The giving you are doing is giving back to you; it feeds your spirit. It is the giving that exhausts that matters. The Meyers-Briggs personality indicator defines an extrovert as a person who is energized by others; an introvert is energized by him- or herself. An introvert gives too much when he or she feels drained, usually by having to "be out there" for a prolonged period. This is tiredness that is not "good" tired, but the kind that rest doesn't restore. Too much of this kind of giving grows out of the belief that your needs are not important. Giving because you believe you don't deserve anything depletes your soul of its spiritual red blood cells.

An extrovert, unlike an introvert, may be able to be around people all day, talking and taking care of matters without feeling the least bit drained. But even an extrovert can exhaust himself by doing it day after day.

There is a need for both personality types. We need extroverts to be out front, organizing, working with groups and making speeches. We need introverts to do the more contemplative thinking, work one on one with folks or be the quiet presence in the organization. Our culture rewards extroverts, which makes many an introvert feel like there is something wrong with them. For an introvert to try to act like an extrovert is draining and not necessary. If you are an introvert who's trying to be an extrovert by running all the time, you will not feel peace until you come to terms with this. We do not need people who ignore themselves to the point of burnout but rather people who take care of themselves so that they may be a positive force in the world.

### 5. Reclaim your spirit

The "e" choices are all about frenzied living. Living at a frantic pace grows out of a distorted perception of events or activities and their relative importance. We see this in bone-tired parents driving their even more bone-tired children to sports events and school activities. Being chronically tired is the consequence of forgetting the essential connection of our spirits to our lives.

While this is not the case the world over, certainly in the United States we can look to our Puritan roots to understand how we came to our belief that, at an unconscious level, idleness is sinful. It sprang from a fundamental belief that at their core, humans were depraved so they would surely do the wrong, selfish or evil thing if not distracted; better not to have the time to do the wrong, selfish or evil thing. The meaning of the belief was, and is, that if you are busy: 1) you are worthwhile and 2) you cannot get into trouble.

Lurking under all this busyness is the fundamental motive for such a feverish pace: Some people, in their deepest reaches, feel they must earn their fundamental human worth.

When you believe this, you can't help but diminish yourself. You function out of the belief that you have no significance. Over time, you will never be able to do enough to earn your worth. You will just get busier, reinforcing your sense of unworthiness.

Yes, you are busy and what you do is important, but which kind of busy are you? Shedding the busyness that drains you and replacing it with unfettered time is how you step onto the path of regaining your spirit. The more you are able to do this, the true nature of the frantic life will become clearer to you. You'll come to recognize that what is within you is substantive and meaningful and that you don't have to validate yourself relentlessly.

### 6. Determine if your need to be busy is how you run from relationships

Vulnerability is the cornerstone of intimacy. If you are a person who is consistently preoccupied you will be consistently unavailable. Your chances of experiencing authentic intimacy are poor. Spouses or friends who do allow themselves to be vulnerable with you, in due course, will feel the imbalance. They will feel exposed and needy. Eventually they will withdraw from you because you never need anything. It is uncomfortable to be in a relationship where a friend or partner is the guru who helps, listens or gives advice, yet won't express personal needs themselves.

When you don't allow yourself to need, you deprive those around you of the opportunity to experience their own value. We feel important when we can comfort someone, help solve a problem, make someone smile. If your friends feel that you don't really need them, it puts them in a one-down position. Being emotionally indebted to someone without the opportunity to reciprocate creates an imbalance; it makes people feel less-than. People don't mind being indebted if they know eventually they have the opportunity give something back. Reciprocating affirms their spirit because they are able to experience their own significance and purpose in creation.

### 7. Practice emotional reciprocity

If you are in a hurry, always running to the next thing, you might actually be avoiding interpersonal connection. If you're always on the go, you don't have time for talking, visiting, listening. All these little acts of familiarity and connection are what lead to friendship. Friendship means you have to give something of yourself and this means you are opening yourself, even if it's ever so slightly, to another person. You might want to ask yourself these questions: What is my busyness-isolation doing for me? Do I lose more than I gain when I don't let others "in?" What is my spirit longing for and why do I hide it from myself?

Stop long enough to notice the efforts other people make towards you and make the same effort with them. Your gift will be the connection which takes place. Another gift will be a reminder that there are other people out there and that, just possibly, you might be overinvolved with your stuff.

If someone brings you a gift, you don't have to get them one. Simply telling them how much you appreciate it and how you've used it is a powerful affirmation of their importance to you. What if you don't feel that way? Find a way to validate them anyway. Wear the ugly tie or use the mug that says "Wrestlemania rules!" Give something of yourself; your time, your attention, your concern. You will receive much more than you give.

### 8. Begin now to admit when you don't know

If you are a Busy Person, you want to be considered important. After all, look at all the stuff you do. You may have a tendency to bluff your way through something because you don't want to admit you don't know; know how to do it, know the answer, know the right people to contact, know the name of a book being discussed . . . it's all the same. If you don't know, then 'they' will think less of you. Your mask is in danger of being removed!

What are people going think if you don't know? The answer is: It doesn't matter. You can't control what people think and sometimes no matter what you say, there is always a possibility they will think badly of you anyway. Or, they may think nothing at all. The point is really about you being comfortable with whoever you are.

You cannot be all things to all people. In fact, plopping down and admitting you can't do it all only makes you more human and others more comfortable.

### 9. Practice asking for help and do something you don't know how to do

This is fairly straightforward and self-explanatory. This does not mean you contrive ways to ask for help. When you realize you can't do something and you reach the point when you would normally begin to overload yourself, STOP! Remind yourself that when you ask for help, you recognize others as valuable and they, in turn, see you as a "real" person, not a snob.

Usually we like being busy with things we know how to do. It shows we are valuable and competent. We certainly wouldn't want to appear like we feel inside—unworthy.

To break that chain, try something new, something you don't know how to do. One of the reasons you chose more "e's" is because you are afraid. You are afraid you aren't good enough, afraid of what others will think, afraid to stop. To countermand this feeling, you end up doing more and more. The sad thing is there are not enough projects and volunteer positions to fill that hole in you.

By being a novice gardener or photographer, you will experience the tenderness and genuine concern of others when you ask for help; they will probably treat you better than you treat yourself. You will learn that you don't have to prove yourself. Instead of rushing from one thing to another, wondering where the time goes, you will learn to enjoy your time. You will learn to enjoy you. You will learn to relate to someone as an equal. You will learn that if you do step out of your comfort zone, the world won't end. Sometimes being strong means being strong enough not to be strong.

### 10. Meditate

I have left this suggestion for last because if you take nothing else away from this section, I would want you to take this: Meditation is the single most significant act you can incorporate in your life to help yourself. You may feel like you are the last person who could meditate and, maybe you are. But it doesn't negate the profound effect this practice will have on your life.

There are hundreds of books and CDs on meditation but I will mention only two here: *Wherever You Go, There You Are,* by Jon Kabat-Zinn and a CD, *The Art of Meditation,* by Daniel Goleman.

Both of these are down-to-earth, practical and easy to follow. Jon Kabat-Zinn is the founder of the Stress Reduction Clinic at the University of Massachusetts; his book shows how simple it is to meditate without a lot of time and trappings. Daniel Goleman who wrote *Emotional Intelligence*, presents the case for meditation and his CD guides you through four types of meditating.

Meditation has been shown not only to reduce stress, but strengthen the immune system and bring about emotional growth.

You cannot afford to not take the time, sometimes just two minutes, to reconnect with yourself, becoming mindful of the moment you are in and the moments you have. If you don't, your busyness and doing will accommodate you with many, many regrets to keep you company in your old age.

Meditation may feel like one more item to add to your list and until you're ready to really hear this, it probably will remain an item on that list. However, please make this note on your list: *Meditation will give me my life back.

Right now I would like you to try something. After reading these instructions, put the book down, close your eyes, take a deep breath expanding your stomach, then breathe out s-l-o-w-l-y through your mouth, each time letting your shoulders drop. Do it two more times, and wait about one minute after your last breath. How do you feel now compared to two minutes ago? You should feel calmer and more grounded. This little exercise that took two minutes has already begun to alter your body's ability to heal.

There are many misconceptions about meditation. It can be deeply religious or not religious at all. It can follow a format or not. You don't have to wear funny clothes or sit in the forest to do it. It is simply a way to break the hypnotic hold our possession- and performance-driven culture has on us. Give it a week . . . it can change your life.

# Epilogue

*And I like you just the way you are.*—Mr. Rogers

This book is about exposing the Myth of Self-Esteem. Because of this myth, many of us think that it's dangerous to drop our protective, disfiguring masks. Yet a myth is, after all, just a myth. It is the boogey-man in the closet. When we finally muster up the courage to tiptoe over and open the door, we find the closet empty. And so it is with you. When you are ready to accept the ugly-beautiful truth that there is messiness and grace in each of us, you will know peace. Amen and shalom.

# Endnotes

1. Walt Whitman, "Song of Myself," Modern American Poetry, ed. Louis Untermeyer (New York: Harcourt, Brace & Co. 1950), p. 46.

2. James Hillman, *The Myth of Family,* Sound Horizons Audio, 1997. Recorded live at the New York Open Center.

3. *The Oxford Dictionary of Quotations* (London: Oxford University Press, 1966) "The Epic of Hades, Marsyas." Sir Lewis Morris.

4. Ernest Kurtz, Katherine Ketcham, *The Spirituality of Imperfection*, (Bantam Books: New York, 1994), p. 5.

5. James Hillman, *The Soul's Code*, (New York: Random House, 1996) p. 4.

6. Deepak Chopra, *The Seven Spiritual Laws of Success* (San Rafael: New World Library, 1994), pp. 10, 9.

7. "Song of Myself," p. 46.

8. William Shakespeare, *The Complete Plays and Poems of William Shakespeare* (Cambridge: Houghton Mifflin Co: The Riverside Press, 1942), Romeo and Juliet, II. 11, p. 166.

9. Thomas Moore, *Care of the Soul*, (New York: Harper Collins, 1992).

10. The New Oxford Annotated Bible, New Revised Standard Version, (New York: Oxford University Press, 1991), Psalm 62, p.725.

11. Thomas Moore, *Care of the Soul*, (New York: Harper Collins, 1992)

12. Ibid.

13. HADASSAH magazine, Portrait: Aaron Feuerstein, by Helen Mintz Belitsky.

14. Fredericksburg (Virginia) *Free Lance-Star*, section E2, May 27, 2000.

15. Clarissa Pinkola Estes, *Women Who Run with the Wolves* (New York: Ballantine, 1995) p. 462.

16. James Hillman, *The Soul's Code*, (New York: Random House, 1996).

17. Ibid., p. 86.

18. Eric Berne, *Games People Play*, (New York: Ballentine Books: 1996).

19. Fredericksburg (Virginia) *Free Lance-Star*, section E2, May 27, 2000.

20. *On Intimacy*, Dr. Harriet Lerner, Sounds True Studios, Boulder, Colorado, 1995.

21. For a list of therapists in your area who are relationship specialists, visit the American Association for Marriage and Family Therapy at their Web site: www.aamft.org.

22. Thomas Moore, *Care of the Soul,* (New York: Harper Collins, 1992), p. 181.

23. Ibid, p. 186.

24. Daniel Goleman, *Emotional Intelligence,* (New York: Bantam Books, 1995), p. 83–84.

25. Bureau of Labor Statistics: American Time Use Survey Summary. 10/20/2005. Available at: http://www.bls.gov/news.release/atus.nr0.htm.

26. World Tourism Organization, 2005. Average Number of Vacation Days Around the World. Available at: Infoplease; http://www.infoplease.com

27. Herbert Benson, *Timeless Healing*, (New York: Scribner 1996) p. 138.

28. Lao-Tzu, *Tao Te Ching*, trans. Stephen Mitchell (New York: Harper Perennial, 1992), 9.

29. Deepak Chopra, *The Seven Spiritual Laws of Success* (San Rafael: New World Library, 1994), pp. 53–64.

30. Daniel Goleman, *Emotional Intelligence*, p. 27.

31. Lao-Tzu, *Tao Te Ching,* p. 11.

32. Herbert Benson, *Timeless Healing*, p. 146.

33. Lao-Tzu, *Tao Te Ching,* p. 11.

34. The *Washington Post*, Department of Human Behavior Section, "The Christmastime Self-Esteem Paradox," Shankar Vedantum, January 2008.

35. www.forparentsbyparents.com, Descriptive Praise, extract from "How to Be a Better Parent," Cassanran Jardine Vermillion, Vermillion Publishing, October 9, 2003.

36. Kohn, Alfie, *Five Reasons to Stop Saying Good Job, Young Children,* 2001.

37. Ibid.

38. Hans Christian Anderson, *The Princess and the Pea,* illustrated by Edmund Dulac

39. Daniel Goleman, *Emotional Intelligence,* (New York: Bantam Books, 1995), pp. 81–83.

40. Carol Tavis, Elliot Aronson, *Mistakes Were Made (but not by me),* (New York: Harcourt, 2007).

41. Joseph Campbell, *The Power of Myth,* (New York: Doubleday, 1988).

# Index